The Metropolitan Opera Presents

Giacomo Puccini's

La Bohème

The Metropolitan Opera Presents

Giacomo Puccini's

La Bohème

Music by Giacomo Puccini

Libretto by Giuseppe Giacosa and Luigi Illica

Based on the novel *Scènes de la Vie de Bohème*
by Henri Murger

AMADEUS
PRESS
An Imprint of Hal Leonard Corporation

The **Met**
ropolitan
Opera

Published in 2014 by Amadeus Press
An Imprint of Hal Leonard Corporation
7777 West Bluemound Road
Milwaukee, WI 53213

Trade Book Division Editorial Offices
33 Plymouth St., Montclair, NJ 07042

English translation of libretto copyright © 1994 and 2004 by Leyerle Publications, 28 Stanley Street, Mt. Morris, New York 14510. English translation by Nico Castel. Originally published by Leyerle Publications as part of *The Complete Puccini Libretti*, in two volumes. These publications, and others in the Leyerle Opera Libretti series, are available directly from Leyerle's website at www.leyerlepublications.com.

Printed in the United States of America

Book design by Mark Lerner

Library of Congress Cataloging-in-Publication Data is available upon request.

ISBN 978-1-57467-444-6

www.amadeuspress.com

CONTENTS

Metropolitan Opera House.

Lessee,   MAURICE GRAU OPERA CO.

GRAND OPERA

SEASON 1900-1901.

Under the direction of

MR. MAURICE GRAU

SPECIAL NOTICE.

In consequence of the indisposition of MISS FRITZI SCHEFF, the role of
"Musetta" will be sung to-night by MISS OCCHIOLINI.

WEDNESDAY EVENING, DECEMBER 26, 1900,

at 8.15 o'clock,

First Performance at the Metropolitan Opera House of

PUCCINI'S OPERA,

LA BOHEME

(In Italian).

MIMI.	MME. MELBA
MUSETTA	MISS OCCHIOLINI
RODOLFO	MR. SALEZA
MARCELLO	MR. CAMPANARI
SCHAUNARD	MR. GILIBERT
COLLINE	MR. JOURNET
BENOIT	MR. DUFRICHE
ALCINDORO	
PARPIGNOL	MR. MASIERO
Conductor	MR. MANCINELLI

Programme continued on the next page.

MI FAVORITA

KEY WEST CLEAR HAVANA CIGARS.

For sale by PARK & TILFORD, Wholesale and Retail.

THE ONLY SALESROOMS IN GREATER NEW YORK FOR
THE CELEBRATED

PIANOS **SOHMER** PIANOS

ARE NOW LOCATED IN THE NEW SOHMER BUILDING,
FIFTH AVENUE, CORNER 22D STREET.

THE "SOHMER" HEADS THE LIST OF THE HIGHEST GRADE PIANOS.

INTRODUCTION

Four years after its 1896 world premiere in Turin, the Met first presented *La Bohème* while on tour in Los Angeles, with the great Nellie Melba as Mimì. For the next 58 years, the opera never left the repertoire, and since then there have only been a handful of seasons when it was not performed—making it the most frequently staged work in the history of our company. *La Bohème's* moving story of tragic young love and its colorful Parisian setting have been seen in five different Met productions, perhaps most memorably in Franco Zeffirelli's legendary staging. With some of the best-known arias in the repertoire, the opera has served as the debut vehicle for some of the Met's greatest singers: Jussi Björling, Jarmila Novotna, Dorothy Kirsten, Mirella Freni, Luciano Pavarotti, Ileana Cotrubas, and, more recently, Angela Gheorghiu, Roberto Alagna, and Vittorio Grigolo are just a few of the artists who made their first appearances on the Met stage in Puccini's masterpiece. *La Bohème* also inaugurated the series of *Live from the Met* telecasts on PBS in 1977.

With this second volume of the Metropolitan Opera Presents series, we aim to provide readers with a complete introduction to this much-loved opera. In the pages that follow, you will find the full libretto, a synopsis, a detailed program note with historical and musicological background, and the "In Focus" article we include in the Met's house program every night—a brief summary of the essentials on a given opera and its creators that is easy to take in just before the performance starts. Also included is a selection of photographs from the Met Archives, featuring some of the extraordinary artists heard and seen in *La Bohème* throughout its 114-year history at the Met. Whether you experience *La Bohème* at the opera house, as part of our *Live in HD* movie-theater transmissions or radio broadcasts, or as a web stream, we hope this book will give you all the information you need to enjoy and appreciate one of opera's greatest works.

Peter Gelb
General Manager
Metropolitan Opera

To learn more about Met productions, Live in HD *movie-theater transmissions, Met membership, and more, visit metopera.org.*

The Metropolitan Opera Presents

Giacomo Puccini's

La Bohème

Giuseppe Campanari as Marcello, 1900
AIMÉ DUPONT/METROPOLITAN OPERA ARCHIVES

Synopsis

Act I

Paris in the 1830s. In their Latin Quarter garret, the near-destitute artist Marcello and poet Rodolfo try to keep warm on Christmas Eve by feeding the stove with pages from Rodolfo's latest drama. They are soon joined by their roommates—Colline, a young philosopher, and Schaunard, a musician, who brings food, fuel, and funds he has collected from an eccentric student. While they celebrate their unexpected fortune, the landlord, Benoit, comes to collect the rent. Plying the older man with wine, they urge him to tell of his flirtations, then throw him out in mock indignation at his infidelity to his wife. As his friends depart to celebrate at the Café Momus, Rodolfo promises to join them later, remaining behind to try to write. There is another knock at the door; the visitor is a pretty neighbor, Mimì, whose candle has gone out on the drafty stairway. No sooner does she enter than the girl feels faint; after reviving her with a sip of wine, Rodolfo helps her to the door and relights her candle. Mimì realizes she lost her key when she fainted, and as the two search for it, both candles are blown out. In the darkness, Rodolfo finds the key and slips it into his pocket. In the moonlight, the poet takes the girl's shivering hand, telling her his dreams. She then recounts her life alone in a lofty garret, embroidering flowers and waiting for the spring. Rodolfo's friends are heard outside, urging him to join them; he calls back that he is not alone and will be along shortly. Expressing their joy in finding each other, Mimì and Rodolfo embrace and slowly leave, arm in arm, for the café.

Act II

Amid the shouts of street hawkers, Rodolfo buys Mimì a bonnet near the Café Momus and then introduces her to his friends; they all sit down and order supper. The toy vendor Parpignol passes by, besieged by eager children. Marcello's former sweetheart, Musetta, makes a noisy entrance on the arm of the elderly but wealthy Alcindoro. The ensuing tumult reaches its peak when, trying to regain Marcello's attention, Musetta sings a waltz about her popularity. She complains that her shoe pinches, sending Alcindoro off to fetch a new pair. The moment he is gone, she falls into Marcello's arms and tells the waiter to charge everything to Alcindoro. Soldiers march by the café, and as the Bohemians fall in behind, Alcindoro rushes back with Musetta's shoes.

Act III

At dawn on the snowy outskirts of Paris, a customs official admits farm women to the city. Merrymakers are heard within a tavern. Soon Mimì wanders in, searching for the place where Marcello and Musetta now live. When the painter emerges, she tells him of her distress over Rodolfo's incessant jealousy. She says she believes it is best that they part. Rodolfo, who has been asleep in the tavern, wakes and comes outside. Mimì hides nearby, though Marcello thinks she has gone. The poet first tells Marcello that he wants to separate from his sweetheart, citing her fickleness; pressed for the real reason, he breaks down, saying that her coughing can only grow worse in the poverty they share. Overcome with tears, Mimì stumbles forward to bid her lover farewell as Marcello runs back into the tavern upon hearing Musetta's laughter. While Mimì and Rodolfo recall past happiness, Musetta dashes out of the inn, quarreling with Marcello, who has caught her flirting. The painter and his mistress part, hurling insults at each other, but Mimì and Rodolfo decide to remain together until spring.

Act IV

It is several months later. Now separated from their girlfriends, Rodolfo and Marcello lament their loneliness in the garret. Colline and Schaunard bring a meager meal; to lighten their spirits, the four stage a dance, which turns into a mock duel. At the height of the hilarity, Musetta bursts in to tell them that Mimì is outside, too weak to come upstairs. As Rodolfo runs to her aid, Musetta relates how Mimì begged to be taken to her lover to die. The poor girl is made as comfortable as possible, while Musetta asks Marcello to sell her earrings for medicine and Colline goes off to pawn his overcoat, which for so long has kept him warm. Left alone, Mimì and Rodolfo wistfully recall their meeting and their first happy days, but she is seized with violent coughing. When the others return, Musetta gives Mimì a muff to warm her hands and prays for her life. As Mimi peacefully drifts into unconsciousness, Rodolfo closes the curtain to soften the light. Schaunard discovers that Mimì is dead, and when Rodolfo at last realizes it, he throws himself despairingly on her body, repeatedly calling her name.

Fritzi Scheff as Musetta, 1900
AIMÉ DUPONT/METROPOLITAN OPERA ARCHIVES

In Focus

William Berger

Premiere: Teatro Regio, Turin, 1896

La Bohème, the passionate, timeless, and indelible story of love among young artists in Paris, can stake its claim as the world's most popular opera. It has a marvelous ability to make a powerful first impression (even to those new to opera) and to reveal unsuspected treasures after dozens of hearings. At first glance, *La Bohème* is the definitive depiction of the joys and sorrows of love and loss; on closer inspection, it reveals the deep emotional significance hidden in the trivial things (a bonnet, an old overcoat, a chance meeting with a neighbor) that make up our everyday lives.

The Creators

Giacomo Puccini (1858–1924) was immensely popular in his own lifetime, and his mature works remain staples in the repertory of most of the world's opera companies. His operas are celebrated for their mastery of detail, sensitivity to everyday subjects, copious melody, and economy of expression. Puccini's librettists for *La Bohème*, Giuseppe Giacosa (1847–1906) and Luigi Illica (1857–1919), also collaborated with the composer on his two other most enduringly

successful operas, *Tosca* and *Madama Butterfly*. The French author
Henri Murger (1822–1861) drew on his own early experiences as
a poor writer in Paris to pen an episodic prose novel and later a
successful play, *Scènes de la Vie de Bohème*, which became the basis
for the opera.

The Setting

The libretto sets the action in Paris, circa 1830. This is not a random
setting, but rather reflects the issues and concerns of a particular
time and place. After the upheavals of revolution and war, French
artists had lost their traditional support base of aristocracy and
church and were desperate for new sources of income. The rising
bourgeoisie took up the burden of patronizing artists and earned
their contempt in return. The story, then, centers on self-conscious
youth at odds with mainstream society, feeling themselves morally
superior to the rules of the bourgeois (specifically regarding sexual
mores) and expressing their independence with affectations of
speech and dress. The Bohemian ambience of this opera is clearly
recognizable in any modern urban center. *La Bohème* captures this
ethos in its earliest days.

The Music

Lyrical and touchingly beautiful, the score of *La Bohème* exerts a
uniquely immediate emotional pull. Many of the most memorable
melodies in the score are built incrementally, with small intervals
between the notes that carry the listener with them on their lyrical
path. This is a distinct contrast to the grand leaps and dives that
earlier operas often depended on for emotional effect. *Bohème*'s
melodic structure perfectly captures the "small people" (as Puccini called them) of the drama and the details of everyday life.
The two great love arias in Act I seduce the listener, beginning
conversationally, with great rushes of emotion seamlessly woven
into more trivial expressions. Furthermore, the slightest alterations

to a melody can morph the meaning of a thought or an emotion in this score. A change of tempo or orchestration can turn Musetta's famous, exuberant Act II waltz into the nostalgic, bittersweet tenor/baritone duet in Act IV, as the Bohemians remember happier times. Similarly, the "streets of Paris" theme is first heard as a foreshadowing in Act I, when one of the Bohemians suggests going out on the town, hits full flower in Act II, when they (and we) are actually there, and becomes a bitter, actually chilling memory at the beginning of Act III, when it is slowed down and re-orchestrated. It's a bit like Marcel Proust's prose experiments in time and memory, with a great deal more economy.

La Bohème at the Met

La Bohème had its Met premiere while the company was on tour in Los Angeles (the same city where it received its American premiere) in 1900. Nellie Melba sang Mimì and improbably added the mad scene from Donizetti's *Lucia di Lammermoor* as an encore after the final curtain (a practice she maintained for several other performances). This production lasted until 1952, when it was replaced by one designed by Rolf Gerard and directed by Joseph L. Mankiewicz, who insisted his name be removed after a disagreement with some of the singers. The current spectacular production by Franco Zeffirelli was unveiled in 1981 with an impressive cast that included Teresa Stratas, José Carreras, Renata Scotto, Richard Stilwell, and James Morris, with James Levine conducting. *La Bohème* was presented at the Met in 58 consecutive seasons after its first appearance and has been performed in all but six seasons since 1900.

Geraldine Farrar.
(La Bohème)

Geraldine Farrar as Mimì, 1907
METROPOLITAN OPERA ARCHIVES

Program Note

William Livingstone

"Just as *La Bohème* does not leave much impression in the mind of the listeners, it will not leave much impression on the history of our lyric theater." This was the confident judgment of Carlo Bersezio, writing in *La Stampa* about the opera's premiere at the Teatro Regio in Turin on February 1, 1896.

Bersezio accused Puccini of writing *La Bohème* with "great haste and with little attempt at selection or polishing." This was not true. Although Rossini and Donizetti could dash off an opera in two or three weeks, Puccini spent years on each new work. In fact, three turbulent years separated the premieres of his *Manon Lescaut* and *La Bohème*. Shortly after the great success of *Manon Lescaut* in 1893, Puccini happened to meet his friend Ruggero Leoncavallo in a Milan café, and in conversation it was revealed that each of them was at work on an opera based on Henri Murger's autobiographical sketches, *Scènes de la Vie de Bohème*. A bitter quarrel developed, with the result that the two composers became lifelong enemies. It is well documented that Puccini was, indeed, already at work on such an opera, collaborating with the librettists Giuseppe Giacosa and Luigi Illica, who had done some work on the libretto for *Manon Lescaut* (as had Leoncavallo). Sensitive to the criticism of the librettos of his earlier operas, Puccini was extremely demanding of Giacosa and

Illica, so demanding that there were many arguments and angry letters. At one time or another, both librettists wished to resign from the project and had to be placated by Puccini's publisher, Giulio Ricordi. Puccini was equally demanding of himself and spent almost the entire year of 1895 orchestrating *La Bohème*. The result is a work so polished and tightly constructed that it is impossible to cut one line from it.

Great care went into the preparations for the first production, staged in Turin, where *Manon Lescaut* had had its acclaimed premiere. But, despite the expert conducting of the Teatro Regio's newly appointed musical director, the 28-year-old Arturo Toscanini, the opening night of *La Bohème* was less than the "great and sensational success" the rehearsals had led Puccini to expect. The public was not unenthusiastic, but there were only five curtain calls for the composer, and the critics in Turin were brutal. Bersezio found the music too light. He wrote: "This is music which can amuse us, but hardly move us, and even the intensely dramatic finale of the opera does not seem to me adequately colored and dressed with musical forms." He advised Puccini to consider *Bohème* "a momentary error, a brief digression, and to return to the path of true art." The work's lack of "art" bothered other critics as well. In the review in the *Gazzetta del Popolo*, E. A. Berta addressed Puccini directly: "You have indulged your whim of obliging the public to applaud you where and when you wanted. You can be forgiven for doing this once. But in the future, return to the great and difficult battles of art."

Yet there were some critics who could see a future for *La Bohème*. One from Genoa wrote that he foresaw a "triumphal career for this opera," and Alfredo Colombani said in the *Corriere della Sera* in Milan that he admired the flow of the music, at times exuberant and at times heart-rending, and praised Puccini for never seeking "musical effects greater than those which the situations allow." Though Puccini did not receive the great and sensational success he wanted when *La Bohème* was mounted in Rome and Naples a few weeks after the premiere, the breakthrough came on Friday, April 13, 1896, when the opera was staged in Palermo. The audience was delirious and refused to leave the theater until the final scene had been repeated, a response reported in newspapers throughout Italy and elsewhere.

George Bernard Shaw had recognized Puccini as the heir of Verdi when he saw *Manon Lescaut*, but even after the worldwide success of *La Bohème*, there were Italian critics who could not forgive him for his apparent lack of lofty artistic ambitions. By 1915, Italian music commentators were deploring the fact that foreign countries knew Italian music through the work of this old-fashioned melodist, when Italy could boast such intellectual composers as Ildebrando Pizzetti.

In English-speaking countries, *La Bohème* came in for a different sort of criticism. It was first performed in England in Manchester in 1897, and was sung at Covent Garden later that year in English, and in 1899 in Italian. A company from Italy gave the American premiere of *Bohème* in Los Angeles in 1897, and it was first sung in New York at Wallack's Theater the following year. The Metropolitan premiere took place on December 26, 1900. But *La Bohème* offended Victorian morals. A British critic wrote that Murger's work was "hardly suitable for the book of an opera." After the Met premiere, Henry Krehbiel in the *New York Tribune* wrote: "*La Bohème* is foul in subject, and fulminant but futile in its music. Its heroine is a twin sister of the woman of the camellias but Mimì is fouler than Camille, alias Violetta, and Puccini has not been able to administer the palliative which lies in Verdi's music." Even the legendary Hollywood gossip columnist Louella Parsons once managed to take a swipe at it. Reviewing a 1916 nonmusical film based on Murger's book, she commented that *La Bohème* was "woefully bereft of sunshine and smiles."

Audiences have generally been kinder to Puccini. The Italian public quickly grew so fond of *La Bohème* that Leoncavallo's opera on the same subject, premiered a year after Puccini's, never really

had a chance. Anglo-Saxon audiences may not have responded
quite so readily to Puccini's engaging crew of Bohemians, but the
opera was established in English-speaking countries by some no-
table champions—Nellie Melba (who sang Mimì in the first Italian
performance in London and in the Metropolitan premiere), Enrico
Caruso, and Toscanini, among others. Some still resist Puccini's
frank emotionalism, but audiences moved by his musical and dramatic genius have kept *Bohème* among the handful of indispensable
operas. In reviewing the reissue of Sir Thomas Beecham's recording
with Victoria de los Angeles and Jussi Björling, the English critic
Frank Granville Barker cast aside inhibition and wrote: "The man
or woman who is insensitive to the spell of this performance really
isn't fit to live in civilized society, for it is one of the wonders of the
world."

LA BOHEME ACT

Set design for the 1907 production
METROPOLITAN OPERA ARCHIVES

La Boh

Frances Alda as Mimì, 1913
Herman Mishkin/Metropolitan Opera Archives

LA BOHÈME

PERSONAGGI

Mimì: soprano
Musetta: soprano
Rodolfo, poeta: tenore
Marcello, pittore: baritono
Schaunard, musicista: baritono
Colline, filosofo: basso
Benoit, il padrone di casa: basso
Parpignol, venditore ambulante: tenore
Alcindoro, consigliere di stato: basso
Sergente dei doganieri: basso
Doganiere: basso
Studenti, Sartine, Borghesi, Bottegai e Bottegaie, Venditori ambulanti, Soldati, Camerieri da caffè, Ragazzi, Ragazze, ecc.

CHARACTERS

Mimì, a seamstress: soprano
Musetta, a singer: soprano
Rodolfo, a poet: tenor
Marcello, a painter: baritone
Schaunard, a musician: baritone
Colline, a philosopher: bass
Benoit, their landlord: bass

Parpignol, a toy vendor: tenor
Alcindoro, a state councillor: bass
Customs Sergeant: bass
Customs Officer: bass
Students, working girls, townsfolk, shopkeepers, street-vendors,
soldiers, waiters, children

Epoca: 1830 circa. Luogo: Parigi.
The time is circa 1830. The Latin Quarter, Paris.

ATTO PRIMO
ACT I

In soffitta
A garret

(Ampia finestra dalia quale si scorge una distesa di tetti coperti di neve. A destra un camino. Una tavola, un letto, quattro sedie, un cavalletto da pittore con una tela sbozzata: libri sparsi, molti fasci di carte. Rodolfo guarda meditabondo fuori della finestra. Marcello lavora al suo quadro "Il passaggio del Mar Rosso," colle mani intirizzite dal freddo e che egli riscalda alitandovi su di quando in quando.)
(It is Christmas Eve. A large window looks out over a large expanse of snow-covered roofs. A stove, bed, table, chairs, painter's easel and stool are placed about the room. On the easel is a half-finished canvas of the crossing of the Red Sea. There are books and manuscripts everywhere. Rodolfo is thoughtfully looking out the window. Marcello works at his painting. Both men are cold and slap themselves and blow on their hands from time to time to warm themselves.)

MARCELLO
Questo *Mar Rosso* mi ammollisce e assidera
This Sea Red me soaks and freezes

come se addosso mi piovesse in stille.
as if on my back me rained in drops.
(as if it rained on me in drops.)

Per vendicarmi affogo un Faraon!
To avenge myself I drown a Pharaoh!

(a Rodolfo)
(to Rodolfo)
Che fai?
What are you doing?

RODOLFO
Nei cieli bigi guardo fumar dai mille comignoli Parigi,
In the skies gray I see smoking from a thousand chimneys Paris,

(indicando la stufa)
(pointing to the stove)

e penso a quel poltrone d'un vecchio caminetto ingannatore
and I think of that idler of an old stove deceitful
(I look out at the gray skies and the thousand smoking chimneys
in Paris, and I think of that old lazy deceitful stove)

che vive in ozio come un gran signor!
that lives in leisure like a great lord!

MARCELLO
Le sue rendite oneste da un pezzo non riceve.
His wages honest for a while (he) doesn't receive.
(He hasn't received his just wages for a long time.)

RODOLFO
Quelle sciocche foreste che fan sotto la neve?
Those dumb forests, what are they doing under the snow?[1]

MARCELLO
Rodolfo, io voglio dirti un mio pensier profondo:
Rodolfo, I wish to tell you a my thought profound:
(I wish to tell you a profound thought of mine:)

ho un freddo cane![2]
I have a cold dog!
(I'm terribly cold!)

RODOLFO
Ed io, Marcel, non ti nascondo
And I, Marcel, not from you hide

che non credo al sudor della fronte.
that I don't believe in the sweat of the brow.
(And I won't hide from you, Marcel, that I don't believe in the
sweat of the brow.)

MARCELLO
Ho ghiacciate le dita
I have frozen my fingers

quasi ancora le tenessi immollate
as if still them I had plunged

giù in quella gran ghiacciaia
down in that great icebox

che è il cuore di Musetta.
which is the heart of Musetta.
(My fingers are frozen, as if I still had them plunged in that great
big icebox that is Musetta's heart.)

(Lascia sfuggire un lungo sospirone, e tralascia di dipingere.)
(He lets go a long sigh and stops painting, setting down palette and brushes.)

RODOLFO
L'amore è un caminetto che sciupa troppo…
Love is a stove that consumes too much…

MARCELLO
E in fretta…
And in a hurry…

RODOLFO
Dove l'uomo è fascina…
Where man is the kindling…

MARCELLO
E la donna è l'alare…
And the woman is the andiron…

RODOLFO
L'uno brucia in un soffio…
The one burns in a flash…

MARCELLO
E l'altro sta a guardare.
And the other stands by and watches.

RODOLFO
Ma intanto qui si gela...
But meanwhile here we freeze...

MARCELLO
E si muore d'inedia!
And one dies of starvation!

RODOLFO
Fuoco ci vuole...
Fire is needed...

MARCELLO
(afferrando una sedia)
(seizing a chair and preparing to break it up)

Aspetta...sacrifichiam la sedia!
Wait...let's sacrifice the chair!

(Rodolfo impedisce l'atto di Marcello. Ad un tratto dà un grido di gioia.)
(Rodolfo stops Marcello, and suddenly lets go with a great shout of joy:)

RODOLFO
Eureka!
Eureka!

(Rodolfo corre al tavolo e prende un grosso fascio di carte da esso.)
(Rodolfo runs to the table and takes a thick sheaf of papers from it.)

MARCELLO
Trovasti?
Did you find it?

RODOLFO
Sì. Aguzza l'ingegno. L'idea vampi in fiamma.
Yes! Sharpen your wits. The idea let it blaze in flames.

MARCELLO
(additando il suo quadro)
(pointing to the Red Sea)
Bruciamo il *Mar Rosso?*
We burn the Sea Red?
(Shall we burn the Red Sea?)

RODOLFO
No! Puzza la tela dipinta.
No! Stinks the canvas painted.
(No! The painted canvas stinks.)

Il mio drama…l'ardente mio dramma ci scaldi.
My drama, the burning my drama us warm.
(My drama. Let my burning drama warm us.)

MARCELLO
Vuoi leggerlo forse? Mi geli.
You want to read it perhaps? You're freezing me.

RODOLFO
No! In cener la carta si sfaldi
No! In ashes the paper itself flake away

e l'estro rivoli ai suoi cieli.
and inspiration fly back to its heavens.
(No! Let the paper flake away in ashes, and inspiration fly back to its heavens.)

(con tragica enfasi)
(with tragic emphasis)

Al secol gran danno minaccia...
To this century great harm threatens...
(Great harm threatens our century...)

È Roma in periglio!
Is Rome in danger!
(Rome is in danger!)

MARCELLO
Gran cor!
Big heart!
(Magnanimous!)

RODOLFO
(dando Marcello parte del fascio di carte)
(giving Marcello part of the sheaf of papers)

A te l'atto primo.
To you the act first.
(Take the first act.)

MARCELLO
Qua.
Here.

RODOLFO
Straccia.
Tear it up.

MARCELLO
Accendi.
Light it.

(Rodolfo accende quella parte dello scartafaccio buttato sul foco-lare. Poi i due amici prendono delle sedie e seggono, riscaldandosi voluttuosamente.)

(Rodolfo strikes a tinderbox, lights a candle, and goes to the stove with Marcello. Together they set fire to the part of the sheaf of papers thrown in the hearth, and both take chairs and sit, warming themselves voluptuously.)

RODOLFO, MARCELLO
Che lieto baglior!
What happy glow!

(Si apre la porta ed entra Colline, gelato, battendo i piedi. Getta sulla tavola un pacco di libri.)

(The door opens and Colline enters, frozen, numb, stamping his feet, angrily throwing on the table a pack of old books tied with a handkerchief.)

COLLINE
Già dell'Apocalisse appariscono i segni.
Already of the Apocalypse appear the signs.

In giorno di Vigilia non si accettano pegni!
On Christmas Eve (they) don't accept pawning.
(The signs of the Apocalypse are appearing: No pawning is allowed on Christmas Eve.)

(sorpreso)
(interrupting himself, surprised)

Una fiammata!
A flame!

RODOLFO
(to Colline)
Zitto, si dà il mio drama...
Quiet, they're giving my drama...
(Quiet! They're presenting my drama...)

MARCELLO
...al fuoco.
...to the fire.

COLLINE
Lo trovo scintillante.
I find it sparkling.

RODOLFO
Vivo.
Vivid.

(Il fuoco diminuisce.)
(The fire diminishes.)

MARCELLO
Ma dura poco.
But it lasts a short time.

RODOLFO
La brevità, gran pregio.
(The) brevity, great merit.
(Brevity is a great merit.)

COLLINE
(prendendo la sedia lontano da Rodolfo)
(taking the chair away from Rodolfo)
Autore, a me la sedia.
Author, give me the chair.

MARCELLO
Questi intermezzi fan morir d'inedia. Presto!
These intermissions make one die of boredom. Quickly!

RODOLFO
(prende un'altra parte dello scartafaccio)
(taking another part of the sheaf of papers)
Atto secondo.
Act second.
(Second act.)

MARCELLO
(a Colline)
(to Colline)
Non far sussurro.
Don't make (a) whisper.

(Rodolfo straccia parte dello scartafaccio e lo getta sul camino: il fuoco si ravviva. Colline avvicina ancora più la sedia e si riscalda le mani: Rodolfo è in piedi, presso ai due, col rimanente dello scartafaccio.)
(Rodolfo tears another sheaf of papers and throws it into the stove. The flames are revived. Colline draws the chair still closer and warms his hands. Rodolfo stands near the two, with the rest of the sheaf of papers.)

COLLINE
(alla maniera di un critico teatrale)
(in the manner of a theatrical critic)
Pensier profondo!

Thought profound!
(Profound thoughts!)

MARCELLO
Giusto color!
Right color!

RODOLFO
In quell'azzurro guizzo languente
In that blue flicker languishing

sfuma un'ardente scena d'amor.
vanishes an ardent scene of love.
(In that blue flicker an ardent love scene vanishes.)

COLLINE
Scoppietta un foglio.
Crackles a page.
(A page crackles.)

MARCELLO
Là c'eran baci!
There, they were kisses!

RODOLFO
Tre atti or voglio d'un colpo udir!
Three acts now I wish all at once (to) hear!

(Getta al fuoco il resto del manoscritto.)
(He throws the remaining papers into the fire.)

COLLINE
Tal degli audaci l'idea s'integra!
Thus of the bold ones the thought is integrated!
(Thus the thought of the bold becomes integrated!)

TUTTI
ALL
Bello in allegra vampa svanir.
(It's) beautiful in (a) happy flame to vanish.

(Applaudono entusiasticamente: la fiamma dopo un momento diminuisce.)
(They all applaud enthusiastically. The flame diminishes after a few moments.)

MARCELLO
Oh Dio...già s'abbassa la fiamma.
Oh God...already lowers itself the flame.
(Oh God, the flame is lowering already.)

COLLINE
Che vano, che fragile dramma!
What (a) vain, what (a) fragile drama!

MARCELLO
Già scricchiola, increspasi, muore!
Already it's creaking, it's curling up, it's dying!

COLLINE, MARCELLO
Abbasso, abbasso l'autor!
Down with, down with the author!

(Dalla porta di mezzo entrano due Garzoni, portando l'uno provviste di cibi, bottiglie di vino, sigari, e l'altro un fascio di legna. Al rumore, i tre innanzi al camino si volgono e con grida di meraviglia si slanciano sulle provviste portate dal garzone e le depongono sul tavolo. Colline prende la legna e la porta presso il caminetto: comincia a far sera.)

*(Two delivery boys enter through the center door, bringing food supplies,
wine, firewood and cigars, followed by Schaunard, who enters with an air
of triumph, throwing some money on the ground. The Bohemians throw
themselves upon the provisions. Colline takes the wood and carries it over
to the stove. Evening is beginning to fall.)*

RODOLFO
Legna!
Firewood!

MARCELLO
Sigari!
Cigars!

COLLINE
Bordò!
Bordeaux! (wine)

TUTTI
ALL
Le dovizie d'una fiera il destin ci destinò!
The abundance of a fair (the) destiny for us destined!
(Destiny has brought us the abundance of a fair!)

SCHAUNARD
La Banca di Francia per voi si sbilancia.
The Bank of France for you goes broke.

COLLINE
(raccattando gli scudi insieme agli altri)
(picking up the coins along with Rodolfo and Marcello)
Raccatta, raccatta!
Gather up, gather up!

MARCELLO
(incredulo)
(incredulously)
Son pezzi di latta!
They're pieces of tin!

SCHAUNARD
(mostrando uno scudo)
(showing him a coin)
Sei sordo? Sei lippo? Quest'uomo chi è?
Are you deaf? Are you nearsighted? This man, who is he?

RODOLFO
Luigi Filippo![3] **M'inchino al mio Re!**
Louis Philippe! I bow to my king!

TUTTI
ALL
(riferendosi alle monete sparse sul pavimento)
(referring to the coins strewn about the floor)
Sta Luigi Filippo ai nostri piè!
It's Louis Philippe at our feet!

(Schaunard vorrebbe raccontare la sua fortuna, ma gli altri non lo ascoltano. Dispongono ogni cosa sulla tavola e la legna nel camino.)
(Schaunard would like to tell of his good luck, but the others do not listen to him. They arrange everything on the table, and put the firewood in the stove.)

SCHAUNARD
Or vi dirò: Quest'oro, o meglio, argento,
Now you I'll tell: This gold, or better yet, silver,

ha la sua brava istoria.
has its fine history.

RODOLFO
Riscaldiamo il camino!
Let's warm up the stove!

COLLINE
Tanto freddo ha sofferto!
So much cold has (it) suffered!
(The stove has suffered so much cold!)

SCHAUNARD
Un inglese…un signor…Lord o Milord che sia,
An Englishman…a gentleman…Lord or Milord, as may be

volea un musicista…
wanted a musician…

MARCELLO
(gettando via il pacco di libri di Colline dal tavolo)
(throwing Colline's pack of books off the table)
Via! Prepariamo la tavola!
Away! Let's prepare the table!

SCHAUNARD
Io? Volo!
Me? I'm flying!

RODOLFO
L'esca dov'è?
The kindling, where is it?

COLLINE
Là!
There!

MARCELLO
Qua.
Here.

SCHAUNARD
E mi presento. M'accetta, gli domando…
And myself I present. He accepts me, him I ask…

COLLINE
Arrosto freddo!
Roast cold!
(Cold roast!)

MARCELLO
(disponendo il cibo)
(arranging the food)
Pasticcio dolce!
Pastries sweet!
(Sweet pastries!)

SCHAUNARD
…A quando le lezioni?
…At when the lessons?
(When are the lessons?)

Risponde: "Incominciam!"
He answers: "Let us begin!"

"Guardare!" (e un pappagallo m'addita al primo piano)
"Look!" and a parrot he points out to me on the first floor

poi soggiunge:
then he adds:

"Voi suonare finché quello morire!"
"You play until that dies!"

RODOLFO
Fulgida folgori la sala splendida.
Brilliantly shine the hall splendid.
(Let the splendid hall shine brilliantly.)

SCHAUNARD
E fu così: Suonai tre lunghi dì…
And it was thus: I played (for) three long days…

MARCELLO
(accendere le candele e la loro messa sul tavolo)
(lighting the candles and putting them on the table)
Or le candele!
Now the candles!

COLLINE
Pasticcio dolce!
Pastries sweet!

SCHAUNARD
Allora usai l'incanto di mia presenza bella…
Then I used the spell of my appearance beautiful…

Affascinai l'ancella…
I charmed the maid…

MARCELLO
Mangiar senza tovaglia?
Eat without (a) tablecloth?

RODOLFO
Un'idea!
An idea…

MARCELLO, COLLINE
Il *Costituzionali*
The *Constitutional* (a newspaper)

RODOLFO
(aprendolo)
(unfolding it)
Ottima carta…
Excellent paper…

Si mangia e si divora un'appendice!
One eats and one devours a supplement!

SCHAUNARD
Gli propinai prezzemolo…
To it I administered parsley…
(I administered parsley to the parrot…)

Lorito allargò l'ali, Lorito il becco aprì.
Polly spread his wings, Polly his beak opened.

Un poco di prezzemolo, da Socrate morì!
A bit of parsley, like Socrates he died!

(Vedendo che nessuno sta prestando attenzione a lui, afferra Colline,
che sta davanti a lui con un piatto.)
(Seeing that no one is paying any attention to him, he seizes Colline, who
is going past him with a dish.)

COLLINE
Chi?
Who?

SCHAUNARD
(urlando indispettito)
(shouting, annoyed)
Il diavolo vi porti tutti quanti!
May the devil take you, all of you!

(Poi, vedendoli in atto di mettersi a mangiare il pasticcio freddo:)
(Then, seeing that they are about to begin eating the cold pastry:)

Ed or che fate?
And now what are you doing?

(Allarga le mani solennemente sopra la torta.)
(He spreads his hands solemnly over the pie.)

No! Queste cibarie sono la salmeria
No! These foodstuffs are the provisions

pei dì futuri tenebrosi e oscuri.
for (the) days future, tenebrous and dark.
(for future tenebrous and dark days.)

(Mentre parla, si schiarisce la tabella.)
(While he talks, he clears the table.)

Pranzare in casa il dì della Vigilia
To eat at home the day of Christmas Eve

mentre il Quartier Latino le sue vie
while the Latin Quarter its streets

addobba di salsiccie e leccornie?
bedecks with sausages and delicacies?

Quando un olezzo di frittelle
When an aroma of fritters

imbalsama le vecchie strade?
perfumes the old streets?

Là le ragazze cantano contente…
There the girls sing happily…

RODOLFO, MARCELLO, COLLINE
La vigilia di Natal!
The Eve Of Christmas!
(On Christmas Eve!)

SCHAUNARD
Ed han per eco ognuna uno studente!
And they have for echo, each one a student!
(And each one of the girls has a student for an echo.)

Un po' di religione, o miei signori:
A bit of religion, oh my gentlemen:

Si beva in casa, ma si pranzi fuor!
One drinks at home but one eats out!

(Rodolfo chiude la porta a chiave, poi tutti vanno intorno al tavolo e versano il vino. Si bussa alla porta: s'arrestano stupefatti.)
(Rodolfo closes the door, and all sit down at the table and pour wine. They hear a knock and they stop, dumbfounded.)

BENOIT
(di fuori)
(from outside)
Si può?
May I?

MARCELLO
Chi è là?
Who is there?

BENOIT
Benoit.
Benoit.

MARCELLO
Il padrone di casa!
The boss of house!
(The landlord!)

SCHAUNARD
Uscio sul muso!
Door on (his) mug!
(Slam the door in his face!)

COLLINE
(grida)
(shouting)
Non c'è nessuno!
Not there is no one!
(There's no one here!)

SCHAUNARD
È chiuso.
It's locked!

BENOIT
Una parola.
One word.

SCHAUNARD
(dopo essersi consultato cogli altri, va ad aprire)
(after having consulted with the others)
Sola!
One only!

BENOIT
(Entra sorridente: vede Marcello e mostrandogli una carta dice:)
(He enters smiling, sees Marcello and shows him a piece of paper, saying:)
Affitto!
Rent!

MARCELLO
(ricevendolo con grande cordialità)
(with exaggerated solicitude)
Olà! Date una sedia.
Hey! Give (him) a chair.

RODOLFO
Presto!
Quickly!

BENOIT
(cercando di rifiutare)
(trying to refuse)
Non occorre. Vorrei…
It's not necessary. I'd like…

SCHAUNARD
(Insistendo con dolce violenza, lo fa sedere.)
(Using gentle violence, he insists and forces him to sit.)

Segga.
Sit down.

MARCELLO
(gli versa del vino)
(pouring him wine)
Vuol bere?
Do you wish to drink?
(Would you like a drink?)

BENOIT
Grazie.
Thanks.

RODOLFO, COLLINE
Tocchiamo!
Let's touch glasses!
(Let's toast!)

SCHAUNARD
Beva!
Drink!

(Benoit, posando il bicchiere, mostra la carta a Marcello.)
(All drink. Benoit puts down the glass and turns to Marcello, showing him the piece of paper.)

BENOIT
Questo è l'ultimo trimester...
This is the last trimester...
(This is the last quarter of the year...)

MARCELLO
(con ingenuità)
(naively)

E n'ho piacere
About it I'm pleased.
(I'm glad about it.)

BENOIT
E quindi…
And therefore…

SCHAUNARD
(interrompendolo e la ricarica il bicchiere)
(interrupting him and refilling his glass)
Ancora un sorso?
Again a sip?
(Another drink?)

BENOIT
Grazie.
Thanks.

RODOLFO, COLLINE
Tocchiam!
Let's toast!

I QUATTRO
THE FOUR
Alla sua salute!
To your health!

BENOIT
(riprendendo con Marcello)
(resuming with Marcello)
A lei ne vengo perché
To you I come because

il trimestre scorso mi promise…
the trimester past, me you promised…
(I come to you because last quarter you promised me…)

MARCELLO
Promisi ed or mantengo.
I promised and now I keep.
(I promised and now I keep my promise.)

(indica gli scudi sulla tavola)
(showing Benoit the coins on the table)

RODOLFO
(piano a Marcello)
(softly to Marcello)
Che fai?
What are you doing?

SCHAUNARD
(come sopra)
(as above)
Sei pazzo?
Are you crazy?

MARCELLO
(a Benoit, senza guardare gli altri)
(to Benoit, without ignoring the other two)
Ha visto? Or via, resti un momento in nostra compagnia.
You saw? Now then, stay a moment in our company.

Dica: quant'anni ha, caro Signor Benoit?
Tell (us): how old are you, dear Mr. Benoit?

BENOIT
Gli anni? Per carità!
How old? For pity's sake!

RODOLFO
Su e giù la nostra età.
More or less our age?

BENOIT
Di più, molto di più!
More, much more!

(Mentre fanno chiacchierare Benoit, gli riempiono il bicchiere appena egli l'ha vuotato.)
(While they make Benoit chatter, they refill his wine glass no sooner than it is emptied.)

COLLINE
Ha detto su e giù.
He said more or less.

MARCELLO
(abbassando la voce e con tono di furberia)
(lowering his voice, and in a sly tone)
L'altra sera al Mabil l'han colto
The other night at Mabille[4] they caught you

in peccato d'amor.
in a sin amorous.

BENOIT
(a disagio)
(uneasily)
Io?
I?

MARCELLO
Al Mabil…l'altra sera l'han colto. Neghi!
At Mabille…the other night they caught you. Deny it!

BENOIT
Un caso.
By chance.

MARCELLO
(lusingandolo)
(flattering him)
Bella donna!
Beautiful woman!

BENOIT
(mezzo brillo, con subito moto)
(half tipsy, with a quick reaction)
Ah! Molto!
Ah! Very!

SCHAUNARD, RODOLFO
(gli batte una mano sulla spalla)
(slapping him on the shoulder)
Briccone!
Rogue!

COLLINE
(fa lo stesso sull'altra spalla)
(slapping him on the other shoulder)
Seduttore!
Seducer!

MARCELLO
Una quercia, un cannone!
An oak, a cannon!

RODOLFO
L'uomo ha buon gusto.
The man has good taste.

MARCELLO
Il crin ricciuto e fulvo.
Her hair curly and auburn.

SCHAUNARD
Briccon!
Rogue!

MARCELLO
Ei gongolava, arzillo, e pettoruto.
He swaggered, nimble, full-chested.

BENOIT
(ringalluzzito)
(elated)
Son vecchio ma robusto.
I'm old, but robust!

RODOLFO, SCHAUNARD, COLLINE
(con gravità ironica)
(with comic gravity)
Ei gongolava arzuto e pettorillo.
He swaggered, nimbed and full-chestle.[5]

MARCELLO
E a lui cedea la femminil virtù.
And to him surrendered (the) feminine virtue.

BENOIT
(in piena confidenza)
(confiding confidently)

Timido in gioventù, ora me ne ripago!
Timid as a youth, now I'm getting even!

Si sa, è uno svago qualche…
You know, it's a pastime some…

donnetta allegra…e un po…
little woman cheerful…and a bit…

(accenna a forme accentuate)
(indicating with his hands a good womanly shape)

Non dico una balena, o un mappamondo
I don't say a whale, or a globe

o un viso tondo da luna piena,
or a face round like (a) moon full,
(or a round face like a full moon)

ma magra, proprio magra, no, poi no!
but skinny, really skinny, no, really no!

Le donne magre son grattacapi e spesso…sopraccapi…!
The women skinny are tiresome and often…troublesome![6]

E son piene di doglie…per esempio…mia moglie!
And are full of aches…for instance…my wife!

(Marcello, fingendo indignazione, si alza; gli altri lo imitano.)
*(Marcello slams his fist on the table and rises. The others do the same. Benoit
looks at them, utterly amazed.)*

MARCELLO
Quest'uomo ha moglie e sconcie voglie ha nel cor!
This man has (a) wife and obscene desires has in his heart!

SCHAUNARD, COLLINE
Orror!
Horrors!

RODOLFO
E ammorba, e appesta la nostra onesta magion!
And he corrupts and fouls our honest dwelling!

SCHAUNARD, COLLINE
Fuor!
Out!

MARCELLO
Si abbruci dello zucchero!
Let's burn some sugar!
(Let some sugar be burned![7])

COLLINE
Si discacci il reprobo.
Let's drive out the reprobate!
(Let the reprobate be driven out!)

SCHAUNARD
(maestoso)
(majestically)
È la morale offesa…
It's the morality offended…

BENOIT
(allibito, tenta inutilmente di parlare)
(surprised, trying in vain to get a word in)
Io di'…
I sa…
(He is trying to say: **io dico**, which is "I say")

MARCELLO
Silenzio!
Silence!

SCHAUNARD
...che vi scaccia!
...that you drives away!
(It is offended morality that drives you away!)

BENOIT
Miei signori...
My gentlemen...

MARCELLO, SCHAUNARD, COLLINE
Silenzio! Via signore!
Silence! Out, sir!

I QUATTRI
THE FOUR
(spingendo Benoît fuori dalla porta)
(surrounding Benoit and pushing him towards the door)
Via di qua! E buona sera a vostra signoria...ah! ah!
Out of here! And good night to your Lordship...ah! ah!

(Benoit è cacciato fuori.)
(Benoit is thrown out.)

MARCELLO
(chiudendo l'uscio)
(closing the door)
Ho pagato il trimester!
I've paid the trimester!

SCHAUNARD
Al Quartiere Latin ci attende Momus.
At (the) Quarter Latin, us awaits Momus.[8]
(Momus awaits us at the Latin Quarter.)

MARCELLO
Viva chi spende.
Long live he (who) spends.

SCHAUNARD
Dividiamo il bottin!
Let us divide the booty!

(Dividono gli scudi.)
(They divide up the coins left on the table.)

RODOLFO, COLLINE
Dividiam!
Let's divide!

MARCELLO
(presentando uno specchio a Colline)
(presenting a broken mirror to Colline)
Là ci son beltà scese dal cielo.
There, there are beauties descended from Heaven.

Or che sei ricco, bada alla decenza!
Now that you're rich, pay heed to decency!

Orso, ravviati il pelo.
Bear, tidy up your hair.

COLLINE
Farò la conoscenza la prima volta d'un barbitonsore.
I'll make the acquaintance (for) the first time of a barber.

Guidatemi al ridicolo oltraggio d'un rasoio.

Lead me to (the) ridiculous outrage of a razor.

TUTTI
ALL.
Andiam!

Let's go!

RODOLFO
Io resto per terminar l'articolo di fondo del *Castoro*.

I'll stay to finish the leading article for *The Beaver*.

MARCELLO
Fa presto!

Hurry up!

RODOLFO
Cinque minuti, conosco il mestier.

Five minutes, I know the subject.

COLLINE
Ti aspetterem dabbasso dal portier.

We'll wait for you downstairs at the concierge's.

MARCELLO
Se tardi udrai che coro.

If you delay, you'll hear what chorus!
(If you delay, what a chorus you'll hear!)

RODOLFO
(Rodolfo prende un lume ed apre l'uscio. Gli altri escono e scendono la scala.)
(He takes a light, opens the door and the others leave, going down the stairs.)
Cinque minuti.

Five minutes.

SCHAUNARD
Taglia corta la coda al tuo *Castor*!
Cut short the tail of your *Beaver*!

MARCELLO
(di fuori)
(from outside)
Occhio alla scala, tieni alla ringhiera.
Keep your eye on (the) stairs, hold on to the railing.

RODOLFO
(alzando il lume)
(still at the door, holding the light)
Adagio!
Slowly!

COLLINE
(di fuori)
(from outside)
È buio pesto.
It's pitch dark!

SCHAUNARD
(di fuori)
(from outside)
Maledetto portier!
Cursed concierge!

*(**Rumore d'uno che ruzzola.**)*
(The sound of someone tumbling down the stairs is heard.)

COLLINE
Accidenti!
Damn it!

RODOLFO
Colline, sei morto?
Colline, are you dead?

COLLINE
Non ancor!
Not yet!

MARCELLO
(dal basso)
(from below)
Vien presto!
Come quickly!

(Rodolfo chiude l'uscio, pone il lume sulla tavola, e si mette a scrivere. Ma straccia il foglio e getta via la penna.)
(Rodolfo closes the door, puts down the light, clears the table a bit, takes an inkwell and paper, then sits down to write, after putting out the other light which had stayed lit. But finding no inspiration he becomes restless, tears up the paper and throws away the pen.)

RODOLFO
Non sono in vena!
Not I am in (the) mood!

(Bussano timidamente alla porta.)
(A timid knock is heard at the door.)

Chi è là?
Who is there?

MIMÌ
(di fuori)
(from outside)

Scusi.
Excuse me.

RODOLFO
Una donna!
A woman!

MIMÌ
Di grazia, mi si è spento il lume.
Please, to me it has gone out the light.
(Please, my light has gone out.)

RODOLFO
(aprendo)
(running to open)
Ecco!
Here (I am!)

MIMÌ
(sull'uscio, con un lume spento in mano ed una chiave)
(at the door with an extinguished candle and a key in her hands)
Vorrebbe?
Would you?

RODOLFO
S'accomodi un momento.
Come in (for) a moment.

MIMÌ
Non occorre.
It's not necessary.

RODOLFO
(insistendo)
(insisting)

La prego, entri.
Please, come in.

(Entrando, Mimì è presa da soffocazione.)
(Mimì enters and is seized with choking.)

RODOLFO
(premuroso)
(concerned)
Si sente male?
Yourself you feel ill?
(Do you feel ill?)

MIMÌ
No...nulla.
No...nothing.

RODOLFO
Impallidisce!
You're growing pale!

MIMÌ
(preso da tosse)
(seized by coughing)
È il respir...quelle scale...
My breath...those stairs...

(Sviene e Rodolfo è appena a tempo di sorreggerla ed adagiarla su una sedia, mentre dalle mani di Mimì cadono e candeliere e chiave.)
(She faints and her key and candle fall to the floor. Rodolfo barely has time to support her and ease her into a chair.)

RODOLFO
(imbarazzato)
(bewildered)

Ed ora come faccio?
And now how I do?
(What shall I do now?)

(Va a prendere dell'acqua e ne spruzza il viso di lei.)
(He goes to fetch some water and sprinkles Mimì's face with it.)

Così.
Thus!

(guardandola con grande interesse)
(looking at her with keen interest)

Che viso d'ammalata!
What face of a sick girl!

(Mimì rinviene.)
(Mimì comes to.)

Si sente meglio?
Yourself you feel better?
(Do you feel better?)

MIMÌ
(con un filo di voce)
(in a faint voice)
Sì.
Yes.

RODOLFO
Qui c'è tanto freddo, segga vicino al fuoco.
Here it's so cold, sit near the fire.

(La conduce a sedere presso al camino.)
(He makes Mimì get up and leads her to sit down near the stove.)

Aspetti...un po' di vino.
Wait...a little (of) wine.

(Corre alla tavola e ottiene una bottiglia e bicchiere.)
(He runs to the table and gets a bottle and glass.)

MIMÌ
Grazie.
Thanks.

RODOLFO
(Le dà il bicchiere e le versa da bere.)
(giving her the glass and pouring)
A lei.
For you.

MIMÌ
Poco, poco.
Little, little.
(Just a little.)

RODOLFO
Così?
Like this?

MIMÌ
(come lei beve)
(as she drinks)
Grazie.
Thanks.

RODOLFO
(ammirandola)
(admiring her)
(Che bella bambina!)
(What [a] beautiful girl!)

MIMÌ
(levandosi, cerca il suo candeliere)
(rising, looking for her candlestick)
Ora permetta che accenda il lume. È tutto è passato.
Now allow me to light my candle. Is all over.
(Everything is all right now, please allow me to light my candle.)

RODOLFO
Tanta fretta?
So much haste?

MIMÌ
Sì.
Yes.

(Rodolfo accende il lume e glielo dà.)
(Rodolfo lights Mimì's candle and gives it to her without a word.)

Grazie, buona sera.
Thank you, good evening.

RODOLFO
(L'accompagna fino all'uscio. Ritorna subito al lavoro.)
(He accompanies her to the door, then returns immediately to his work.)
Buona sera.
Good evening.

MIMÌ
(Mimì esce, poi riappare sull'uscio.)
(She leaves, then reappears at the door.)
Oh! sventata! La chiave della stanza,
Oh! foolish me! The key of the room,

dove l'ho lasciata?
where have I it left?
(Oh foolish me, where have I left the key to my room?)

RODOLFO
Non stia sull'uscio: il lume vacilla al vento.
Don't stay at the door, the flame flickers in the wind.

(Il lume di Mimì si spegne.)
(Mimì's candle goes out.)

MIMÌ
Oh Dio! Torni ad accenderlo.
Oh God! Again light it.
(Oh God! Light it again.)

(Rodolfo accorre colla sua candela, ma avvicinandosi alla porta anche il suo lume si spegne e la camera rimane buia.)
(Rodolfo runs with his candle to relight Mimì's but as he nears the door, his light also goes out [or is blown out by him], and the room turns very dark.)

RODOLFO
Oh Dio! Anche il mio s'è spento.
Oh God! Also mine has gone out!

MIMÌ
Ah! E la chiave ove sarà?
Ah! And the key, where can it be?

(Avanzandosi a tentoni, incontra il tavolo e vi depone il suo candeliere.)
(Groping her way she finds the table and puts her candlestick down on it.)

RODOLFO
(Si trova presso la porta e la chiude.)
(He is near the door and closes it.)
Buio pesto!
Pitch dark!

MIMÌ
Disgraziata!
Unlucky me!

RODOLFO
Ove sarà?
Where can it be?

MIMÌ
(confuso)
(confused)
Importuna è la vicina.
Bothersome is the neighbor.
(Your neighbor is being a nuisance.)

RODOLFO
Ma le pare!
Not at all!

MIMÌ
Importuna è la vicina…
Bothersome is the neighbor…

RODOLFO
Cosa dice, ma le pare!
What do you say, not at all!

MIMÌ
Cerchi.
Look for (it).

RODOLFO
Cerco.
I'm looking.

(Cercano, tastando il pavimento colle mani.)
(Mimì looks for the key on the floor, dragging her feet, and Rodolfo does the same.)

MIMÌ
Ove sarà?
Where can it be?

RODOLFO
(Trova la chiave, l'intasca.)
(He finds it and puts it into his pocket.)
Ah!

MIMÌ
L'ha trovata?
It have you found?

RODOLFO
No!

MIMÌ
Mi parve…
To me it seemed…
(It seemed to me…)

RODOLFO
In verità!
In truth!
(Honestly!)

MIMÌ
Cerca?
Are you looking?

RODOLFO
Cerco!
I'm looking!

(Guidato dalla voce di Mimì, Rodolfo finge di cercare mentre si avvicina ad essa. Poi colla sua mano incontra quella di Mimì e l'afferra.)
(Guided by Mimì's voice, Rodolfo pretends to be looking as he comes closer to her. Mimì bends and searches, groping on the ground. Rodolfo's hand meets Mimì's hand and clutches it.)

MIMÌ
(sorpresa)
(surprised, getting up)
Ah!

RODOLFO
(tiene sempre la mano di Mimì)
(holding Mimì's hand)
Che gelida manina, se la lasci riscaldar.
What icy little hand, let it be warmed.

Cercar che giova? Al buio non si trova.
Searching, what's the use? In the dark not it we find.
(What an icy little hand, let me warm it. What is the use of searching? We can't find it in the dark.)

Ma per fortuna è una notte di luna
But by good luck it's a night of moon
(But fortunately it's a moonlit night)

e qui la luna l'abbiamo vicina.
and here the moon, we have it near.

Aspetti, signorina, le dirò con due parole
Wait, miss, to you I'll tell in two words

chi son, chi son, e che faccio, come vivo. Vuole?
who I am, and what I do, how I live. Would you like that?

(Mimì tace.)
(Mimì is silent.)

Chi son? Chi son? Sono un poeta. Che cosa faccio? Scrivo.
Who am I? I'm a poet. What thing do I? I write.
(Who am I? I'm a poet. What do I do? I write.)

E come vivo? Vivo.
And how do I live? I live!

In povertà mia lieta scialo da gran signore
In poverty mine happy I squander like a great Lord
(In my happy poverty I squander like a great Lord)

rime ed inni d'amore.
rhymes and hymns of love.

Per sogni e per chimere e per castelli in aria
For dreams and for chimeras and for castles in the air

l'anima ho milionaria.
the soul I have millionaire.
(When it comes to dreams and fantasies or for castles in the air I
have a millionaire's soul.)

Talor dal mio forziere
At times from my coffer

ruban tutti i gioielli due ladri: gli occhi belli.
steal all the jewels two thieves: the eyes beautiful.
(all my jewels are stolen by two thieves: two beautiful eyes.)

V'entrar con voi pur ora
They entered (here) with you just now
(The thieves, your beautiful eyes, entered here just now)

ed i miei sogni usati,
and my dreams familiar

e i bei sogni miei tosto si dileguar!
and the beautiful dreams mine quickly disappeared!

Ma il furto non m'accora
But the theft doesn't grieve me

poiché, poiché v'ha preso stanza la speranza!
because has taken (their) place the hope!
(because hope has taken their place!)

Or che mi conoscete parlate voi,
Now that me you know, speak yourself,

deh parlate, chi siete? Vi piaccia dir!
come speak, who are you? Would it please you to tell!

Enrico Caruso as Rodolfo, 1915
Herman Mishkin/Metropolitan Opera Archives

Claudia Muzio as Mimì, 1919
HERMAN MISHKIN/METROPOLITAN OPERA ARCHIVES

Nannette Guilford as Musetta, 1924
HERMAN MISHKIN/METROPOLITAN OPERA ARCHIVES

Grace Moore as Mimì, 1928
HERMAN MISHKIN/METROPOLITAN OPERA ARCHIVES

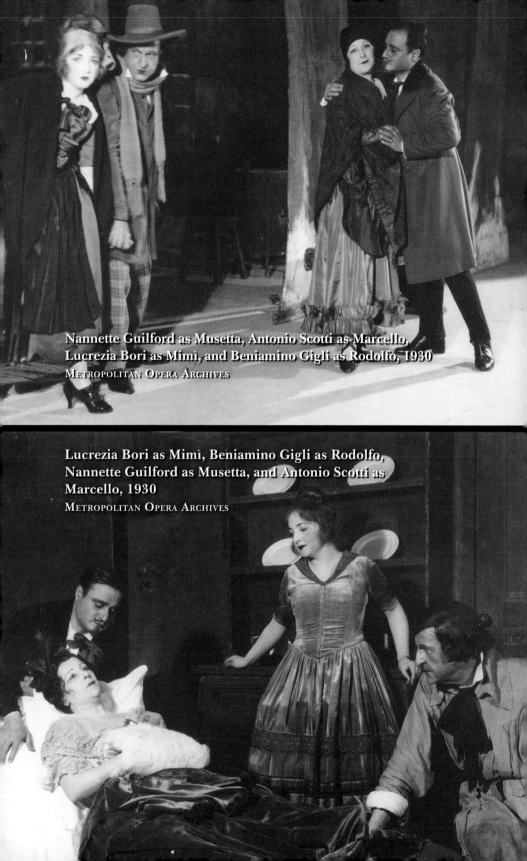

Nannette Guilford as Musetta, Antonio Scotti as Marcello, Lucrezia Bori as Mimì, and Beniamino Gigli as Rodolfo, 1930
METROPOLITAN OPERA ARCHIVES

Lucrezia Bori as Mimì, Beniamino Gigli as Rodolfo, Nannette Guilford as Musetta, and Antonio Scotti as Marcello, 1930
METROPOLITAN OPERA ARCHIVES

Jussi Björling as Rodolfo, 1938
Metropolitan Opera Archives

Bidú Sayão as Mimì, 1940
METROPOLITAN OPERA ARCHIVES

Licia Albanese as Mimì, 1940
METROPOLITAN OPERA ARCHIVES

MIMÌ
Sì, mi chiamano Mimì,
Yes, me they call Mimì,

ma il mio nome è Lucia.
but my name is Lucia.

La storia mia è breve.
The story mine is brief.

A tela o a seta ricamo in casa e fuori.
On cloth or on silk I embroider at home or away.

Son tranquilla e lieta
I'm calm and happy

ed è mio svago far gigli e rose.
and it is my pastime to make lilies and roses.

Mi piaccion quelle cose che han sì dolce malia,
Me please those things that have such sweet magic,

che parlano d'amor, di primavere,
that speak of love, of springtimes,

che parlano di sogni e di chimere,
that speak of dreams and of chimeras,

quelle cose che han nome poesia.
those things that have (the) name poetry.

Lei m'intende?
You understand me?

RODOLFO
Sì.
Yes.

MIMÌ
Mi chiamano Mimì, il perché, non so.
Me they call Mimì, the reason, I don't know.
(They call me Mimì but I don't know why.)

Sola, mi fo il pranzo da me stessa.
Alone me I make the meals by myself.
(I make my meals by myself alone.)

Non vado sempre a messa
Not go I always to Mass
(I do not always go to Mass)

ma prego assai il Signor.
but I pray much (to) the Lord.

Vivo sola, soletta.
I live alone, all alone.

Là in una bianca cameretta
There in a white little room

guardo sui tetti e in cielo.
I look over the roofs and into (the) sky.

Ma quando vien lo sgelo
But when comes the thaw

il primo sole è mio,
the first sun is mine,

il primo bacio dell'aprile è mio!
the first kiss of April is mine!

Il primo sole è mio.
The first sun is mine!

Germoglia in un vaso una rosa…
Blossoms in a vase a rose…
(A rose blossoms in a vase…)

Foglia a foglia l'aspiro!
Leaf by leaf it I observe!

Così gentil è il profumo d'un fior!
So delicate the perfume of a flower!

Ma i fior ch'io faccio, ahimè!…
But the flowers that I make, alas!…

I fior ch'io faccio, ahimè, non hanno odore.
The flowers that I make, alas, don't have (a) fragrance!

Altro di me non le saprei narrare:
Else about me not you I could tell:
(I wouldn't know what else to tell you about myself:)

Sono la sua vicina che la vien
I am your neighbor who to you comes

fuori d'ora a importunare.
at odd hours to bother.
(I'm your neighbor who comes to bother you at an odd hour.)

SCHAUNARD
(dal cortile)
(from the courtyard)
Ehi! Rodolfo!
Hey! Rodolfo!

COLLINE
Rodolfo!

(Alle grida degli amici, Rodolfo s'impazienta.)
(At the cries of his friend, Rodolfo loses his patience.)

MARCELLO
Olà! Non senti! Lumaca!
Hello! Can't you hear! (you) Snail!

COLLINE
Poetucolo!
Poetaster!

SCHAUNARD
Accidenti al pigro!
Damned that lazy one!

(Rodolfo, impaziente, va alla finestra per rispondere. Dalla finestra aperta entrano i raggi lunari, rischiarando la camera.)
(More and more impatient, Rodolfo gropes his way to the window, and leans out to talk to his friends who are below in the courtyard. The moonlight shines in through the open window, lighting the room.)

RODOLFO
(alla finestra)
(at the window)
Scrivo ancora tre righi a volo.
I'll write another three lines in haste.

MIMÌ
(avvicinandosi un poco alla finestra)
(coming close to the window)
Chi sono?
Who are they?

RODOLFO
Amici.
Friends.

SCHAUNARD
Sentirai le tue.
You'll get an earful!

MARCELLO
Che te ne fai lì solo?
What are you doing there alone?

RODOLFO
Non son solo, siamo in due.
I am not alone, we are two.

Andate da Momus, tenete il posto; ci saremo tosto.
Go to Momus, hold the place; there we'll be soon.
(Go to Momus and hold a place. We'll be there soon.)

(Rimane alla finestra, onde assicurarsi che gli amici se ne vanno.)
(He stays at the window to reassure himself that his friends are leaving.)

MARCELLO, SCHAUNARD, COLLINE
Momus, zitti e discreti andiamocene via…
Momus, quiet and discreet, let's go away…

MARCELLO
Trovò la poesia.
He found (the) poetry.

(Si spengono.)
(They go off.)

(Rodolfo volgendosi scorge Mimì avvolta come da un nimbo di luce,
e la contempla, estatico.)
(Mimì is still by the window in such a position that her face is illuminated
by the moonlight. Turning, Rodolfo sees Mimì as if wrapped in a halo of
light, and he contemplates her in great ecstasy.)

RODOLFO
O soave fanciulla!
Oh gentle maiden!

O dolce viso, di mite circonfuso alba lunar,
Oh sweet face, with gentle surrounding dawn lunar,
(Oh sweet face surrounded by gentle moonlight,)

in te ravviso il sogno
in you I see the dream

ch'io vorrei sempre sognar!
that I would wish always to dream.

MIMÌ
Ah! Tu sol comandi, Amor!
Ah! You alone command, Love!

RODOLFO
Fremon già nell'anima le dolcezze estreme.
Tremble already in the soul the sweetnesses extreme.
(Sublime sweetness already trembles in my soul.)

MIMÌ
Oh! come dolci scendono le sue lusinghe al core!
Oh! How sweetly descend his compliments to my heart!

Tu sol comandi, Amore!
You alone command, Love!

RODOLFO
Fremon dolcezze estreme,
Tremble (the) sweetnesses extreme,

nel bacio freme amor!
in the kiss trembles love!
(love trembles in a kiss.)

(Rodolfo la bacia.)
(He kisses her.)

MIMÌ
No, per pietà!
No, for pity's sake!

RODOLFO
Sei mia!...
You're mine!...

MIMÌ
V'aspettan gli amici...
Await you the friends...
(Your friends are awaiting you...)

RODOLFO
Già mi mandi via?
Already me you're sending away?

MIMÌ
Vorrei dir...ma non oso.
I would like to say...but I don't dare...

RODOLFO
Di'...
Say (it)...

MIMÌ
(con graziosa furberia)
(with charming slyness)
Se venissi con voi?
If I came with you?

RODOLFO
Che...? Mimì!
What...? Mimì!

(insinuante)
(with enticing intention)

Sarebbe così dolce restar qui.
It would be so sweet to stay here.

C'è freddo fuori...
It's cold outside...

MIMÌ
Vi starò vicina...!
To you I'll be close...!

RODOLFO
E al ritorno?
And when we return?

MIMÌ
Curioso!
Curious!

RODOLFO
Dammi il braccio, o mia piccina…
Give me your arm, my little one…

MIMÌ
Obbedisco, signor!
I obey, sir!

RODOLFO
Che m'ami, di'…
That you love me, say it!

MIMÌ
Io t'amo!
I love you!

(mentre escono)
(They leave.)

MIMÌ, RODOLFO
Amor!
Love!

FINE DI ATTO I
END OF ACT I

ATTO SECONDO
ACT II

Al Quartiere Latino
The Latin Quarter

(Un piazzale con botteghe di ogni genere. Da un lato il Caffè Momus.
Nella folla si aggirano Rodolfo e Mimì. Colline presso alla bottega di
una rappezzatrice. Schaunard sta comprando una pipa e un corno.
Marcello è spinto qua e là dalla gran folla. È sera. La Vigilia di
Natale.)

(Later that evening in a big square with shops and vendors of every sort
bustling with Christmas Eve activity. To one side is the Café Momus. Rodolfo
and Mimì stroll among the crowd. Colline is near a rag shop, Schaunard at
a junk dealer haggling over a horn and a pipe. Marcello is being pushed
around by the big and varied crowd of townspeople, soldiers, boys, girls,
seamstresses, gendarmes, etc. The shops are decked with lanterns and glowing
lights, which illuminate the entrance of the Café Momus. It is overcrowded,
with some people forced to sit on a table outside.)

I VENDITORI
THE VENDORS
(sul limitare delle loro botteghe)
(at the doors of their shops)
Aranci, datteri, caldi i marroni!
Oranges, dates, hot the chestnuts!

Ninnoli, croci, torroni, panna montata!
Trinkets, crosses, nougats, whipped cream!

Oh! la crostata! Caramelle!
Oh! The pie! Candies!

LA FOLLA
THE CROWD
Quanta folla, che chiasso!
What (a) crowd, what noise!

I VENDITORI
THE VENDORS
Fiori alle belle! Fringuelli, passeri!
Flowers for the beauties! Finches, sparrows!

LA FOLLA
THE CROWD
Su, corriam! Stringiti a me!
Up, let's run, Hold on tightly to me!

I VENDITORI
THE VENDORS
Late di cocco! Panna, torroni!
Milk of cocoanut! Cream, nougats!

LA FOLLA
THE CROWD
Quanta folla! Su, partiam! Date il passo!
What (a) crowd! Come, let's leave! Make way!

AL CAFFÈ
AT THE CAFÉ
Presto qua! Camerier! Un biccchier!
Quickly here! Waiter! A glass!

Corri! Birra! DA ber!
Run! Beer! Something to drink!

LA MADRE
THE MOTHER
(per la sua giovane figlia)
(to her young daughter)
Emma, quando ti chiamo!
Emma, when I you call!
(Emma, when I call you…!)

AL CAFFÈ
AT THE CAFÉ
Dunque? Un caffè! Da ber! Giubbe! Carote!
Well? A coffee! Something to drink! Coats! Carrots!

MONELLI
URCHINS
Voglio una lancia!
I want a lance!

SCHAUNARD
(soffiando nel corno e cavandone note strane)
(blowing into a horn producing some strange notes)
Falso questo *Re*! Pipa e corno quant'è?
False this *Re*! Pipe and horn, how much?
(This D is off!)

(A braccio con Mimì, attraversa la folla avviato al negozio della modista.)
(Rodolfo and Mimì, arm in arm, cross through the crowd, heading for the milliner's shop.)

COLLINE
(dalla rappezzatrice che gli sta cucendo un zimarrone usato che egli ha appena comprato)
(at the shop of a rag dealer, who is mending the lapel of a big coat he has just bought)
È un poco usato...
It's a bit worn...

RODOLFO
Andiam...
Let's go...

MIMÌ
Andiam per la cuffietta?
Are we going for the bonnet?

COLLINE
...ma è serio e a buon mercato...
...but it's sober and cheap...
(The coat is a bit worn, but it's sober and cheap.)

(Paga, poi distribuisce con giusto equilibrio i libri dei quali è carico nelle molte tasche dello zimarrone.)
(He pays and, with the proper balance, distributes the books he is carrying into the many pockets of the long coat.)

RODOLFO
Tienti al mio braccio stretta...
Hold on to my arm tightly...

MIMÌ
A te mi stringo...
To you I hold on tightly...

MIMÌ, RODOLFO
Andiam!
Let's go!

(Entrano dalla modista.)
(They go into the milliner's shop.)

MARCELLO
(tutto solo in mezzo alla folla, con un involto sotto il braccio, occhieggiando le donnine che la folla gli getta quasi fra le braccia)
(all alone in the midst of the crowd, with a package under his arm, ogling the young girls, who are almost pushed into his arms by the pushing crowd)
Io pur mi sento in vena di gridar:
I also myself feel in (the) mood to shout:

Chi vuol, donnine allegre, un po' d'amor?
Who want, girls merry, a bit of love?
(Merry girls! Who wants a bit of love?)

VENDITORI
THE VENDORS
Datteri! Trote! Prugne di Tours!
Dates! Trout! Plums from Tours!

MARCELLO
Facciamo insieme… Facciamo a vendere e a comprar!
Let's play together…Let's play at selling and buying!

UN VENDITORE
ONE VENDOR
Prugne di Tours!
Plums from Tours!

MARCELLO
Io do ad un soldo il vergine mio cuor!
I'll give for a *sou* the virgin my heart!
(I'll give my virgin heart away for one *sou*!)

(La folla si estende lungo le strade adiacenti. I negozi sono pieni di clienti che vanno e vengono. Nel Café vi è un vivace costante di persone che vanno e vengono.)
(The crowd spreads out along the adjacent streets. The stores are full of customers who come and go. In the Café there is a constant bustling of people coming and going.)

SCHAUNARD
(Va a gironzolare avanti al caffè Momus aspettandovi gli amici: intanto armato della enorme pipa e del corno da caccia guarda curiosamente la folla.)
(He comes and saunters in front of the Café Momus, awaiting his friends. Meanwhile, armed with his huge pipe and hunting horn, he looks over the crowd, curiously.)
Fra spintoni e pestate accorrendo affretta
Amid shoves and trampling running hurries

la folla e si diletta
the crowd and itself delights

nel provar voglie matte…insoddisfatte…
in experiencing pleasures mad…unsatisfied…
(The hurrying, running crowd delights in experiencing mad, unsatisfied pleasures amid shovings and tramplings.)

VENDITORI DONNE
WOMEN VENDORS
Ninnoli, spillette, datteri e caramelle!
Trinkets, brooches, dates and candies!

VENDITORI MALE
MALE VENDORS
Fiori alle belle!
Flowers for the beauties!

COLLINE
(Se ne viene al ritrovo, agitando trionfalmente un vecchio libro.)
*(He comes to the meeting place wrapped in his big coat, which is a bit long
for him and makes folds around him like a Roman toga. He triumphantly
waves an old book.)*
Copia rara, anzi unica; la grammatica Runica!
Copy rare, indeed unique; the grammar Runic!
(An indeed rare and unique copy of a Runic grammar![1])

SCHAUNARD
(sopraggiunta in quel momento dietro Colline, di compassione per lui)
(coming up at that moment behind Colline, with compassion for him)
Uomo onesto!
Man honest!
(Honest man!)

MARCELLO
(arrivando al caffè Momus grida a Schaunard e Colline)
(arriving at the Café Momus, finding Schaunard and Colline there)
A cena!
To dinner!

SCHAUNARD AND COLLINE
Rodolfo?

MARCELLO
Entrò da una modista.
He went in at the milliner's.

(Colline, Schaunard e Marcello escono dal caffè portando fuori una tavola; li segue un cameriere colle seggiole; i borghesi al tavolo vicino, infastiditi dal baccano che fanno i tre amici, dopo un po' di tempo s'alzano e se ne vanno. S'avanzano di nuovo Rodolfo e Mimì, questa osserva un gruppo di studenti. Rodolfo e Mimì escono dalla bottega.)
(Marcello, Schaunard and Colline go into the Café Momus, but they come out almost at once, annoyed by the great crowd, which is noisily jammed inside. They carry out a table, and a waiter follows them, not at all surprised at their bizarre desire to dine outside. The bourgeois at a nearby table, annoyed by the noise that the three are making, leave. Rodolfo and Mimì come out of the shop.)

RODOLFO
Vieni, gli amici aspettano.
Come, the friends are waiting.

VENDITORI
SOME VENDORS
Panna montata!
Whipped cream!

MIMÌ
Mi sta ben questa cuffietta rosa?
Me it becomes, this bonnet pink?
(Does this pink bonnet become me?)

MONELLI
URCHINS
Latte di cocco!
Milk of cocoanut!

VENDITORI
SOME VENDORS
Oh! La crostata! Panna montata!
Oh! The pie! Whipped cream!

AL CAFFÈ
AT THE CAFÈ
Camerier! Un bicchier!
Waiter! A glass!

RODOLFO
Sei bruna, e quel color ti dona.
You're dark, and that color suits you.
(You're a brunette and that color suits you.)

AL CAFFÈ
AT THE CAFÈ
Presto, olà! Ratafià!
Quickly, hello! Ratafià!²

MIMÌ
(guardando verso la bottega)
(looking regretfully towards the milliner's shop)
Bel vezzo di corallo.
Beautiful necklace of coral!

RODOLFO
Ho uno zio milionario.
I have an uncle millionaire.
(I have a millionaire uncle.)

Se fa senno il buon Dio
If comes to his senses the good Lord
(If the good Lord comes to this senses)

voglio comprarti un vezzo assai più bel!
I want to buy you a necklace much more beautiful!

BORGHESI
BOURGEOIS
Facciam coda alla gente!
Let's make queue to the people!
(Let's follow the people in a line!)

Ragazze, state attente!
Girls, watch out!

LA FOLLA
THE CROWD
Che chiasso! Quanta folla!
What noise! What a crowd!

BORGHESI
BOURGEOIS
Pigliam via Mazzarino! Io soffoco, partiamo!
Let's take Via Mazzarino! I'm suffocating, let's leave!

Vedi il caffè è vicin! Andiam là, da Momus!
See, the café is near. Let's go there to Momus!

RODOLFO
(con dolce rimprovero, a Mimì)
(suddenly, seeing Mimì looking at someone, turning suspiciously)
Chi guardi?
Whom are you looking at?

COLLINE
Odio il profano volgo al par d'Orazio.[3]
I hate the vulgar crowd just as Horace (did).

MIMÌ
Sei geloso?
Are you jealous?

RODOLFO
All'uom felice sta il sospetto accanto.
To the man happy is the suspicion near.
(Suspicion is always near a happy man.)

SCHAUNARD
Ed io quando mi sazio vo' abbondanza di spazio...
And I when I myself sate I want abundance of space...
(And when I sate myself, I want a lot of space.)

MIMÌ
Sei felice?
Are you happy?

MARCELLO
(al cameriere)
(to the waiter)
Vogliamo una cena prelibata.
We want a dinner special.
(We want a special dinner.)

RODOLFO
Ah, sì, tanto!
Ah yes, so much!

MARCELLO
(al cameriere)
(to the waiter)
Lesto!
Quickly!

SCHAUNARD
Per molti!
For many!

RODOLFO
E tu?
And you?

MIMÌ
Sì, tanto!
Yes, so much!

STUDENTI E SARTINE
SERVANT GIRLS, STUDENTS
Là, da Momus! Andiam!
There, to Momus! Let's go!

MARCELLO, COLLINE, SCHAUNARD
Lesto!
Quickly!

(Rodolfo e Mimì s'avviano al Caffè Momus)
(Rodolfo and Mimì join the friends.)

VOCE DI PARPIGNOL
PARPIGNOL
(in lontananza)
(from the distance, approaching)
Ecco i giocattoli di Parpignol!
Here are the toys of Parpignol!

RODOLFO
(Si unisce agli amici e presenta loro Mimì.)
(arriving with Mimì)

Due posti!
Two places!

COLLINE
Finalmente!
Finally!

RODOLFO
Eccoci qui! Questa è Mimì, gaia fioraia.
We are here. This is Mimì, happy flower maker.

Il suo venir completa la bella compagnia,
Her coming completes the lovely company,

perché…perché son io il poeta…essa la poesia.
because…because I am the poet…she, the poetry.

Dal mio cervel sbocciano i canti,
From my brain blossom the songs,

dalle sue dita sbocciano i fior,
from her fingers blossom the flowers,

dall'anime esultanti sboccia l'amor!
from souls exultant blossoms love!

MARCELLO
(ironico)
(ironically)
Dio, che concetti rari!
Lord! What concepts rare!
(Lord! What rare concepts!)

COLLINE
Digna est intrari.
(LATIN: *She's worthy of entering [our company].*)

SCHAUNARD
Ingrediat si necessit.
(LATIN: *Let her become part of us, if it's necessary.*)

COLLINE
Io non do che un *accessit*![4]
I won't give but an *accessit*! (Latin for "I agree")

VOCE DI PARPIGNOL
PARPIGNOL
Ecco i giocattoli di Parpignol!
Here are the toys of Parpignol!

COLLINE
(vedendo il cameriere gli grida con enfasi)
(with romantic emphasis, to the waiter)
Salame!
Salami!

(Arriva nel piazzale Parpignol, spingendo un carretto tutto a fronzoli e fiori.)
(A cart filled with toys appears, pushed along by Parpignol.)

RAGAZZI E BAMBINE
BOYS AND GIRLS
Parpignol! Ecco Parpignol! Col carretto tutto a fior!
Parpignol! Here's Parpignol! With the cart all flowers!

Voglio la tromba, il cavallin, il tambur, tamburel,
I want the trumpet, the horsey, the drum, tambourine,

Voglio il cannon, voglio il frustin,
I want the cannon, I want the whip,

dei soldati il drappel.
of the soldiers the troop.[5]
(the troop of soldiers.)

(Il cameriere presenta la lista delle vivande, che passa nelle mani dei quattro amici, guardata con una specie di ammirazione e analizzata profondamente.)
(The waiter shows the four friends the menu, which passes from hand to hand, is greatly admired and analyzed in great depth.)

SCHAUNARD
Cervo arrosto!
Stag roast!

MARCELLO
Un tacchino!
A turkey!

SCHAUNARD
Vin del Reno!
Wine of the Rhine!
(Rhine wine!)

COLLINE
Vin da tavola!
Wine of table!
(House wine!)

SCHAUNARD
Aragosta senza crosta!
Lobster without shell!

MAMME
MOTHERS
(Rimproverare, corrono presso le grida dei bambini, cercando invano di farli lontano da Parpignol.)
(Scolding, they run up at the cries of the children, trying in vain to get them away from Parpignol.)
Ah! razza di furfanti indemoniati,
Ah! Bunch of rascals devilish,

che ci venite a fare in questo loco?
what do you come to do in this place?
(what are you coming to this place for?)

A casa! a letto! Via, brutti sguaiati!
Home! To bed! Off! Nasty bawlers!

Gli scappellotti vi parranno poco!
The slaps to you will seem few!
(The slaps you will get will be too few for the way you're behaving!)

UN RAGAZZO
ONE BOY
Vo' la tromba, il cavallin!
I want the trumpet, the little horse!

(Le mamme, intenerite, si decidono a comperare da Parpignol, i ragazzi saltano di gioia, impossessandosi dei giocattoli. Parpignol prende giù per via Commedia. I ragazzi e le bambine allegramente lo seguono, marciando e fingendo di suonare gli strumenti infantili acquistati loro.)
(The children don't wish to leave. One of them bursts out weeping. His mother seizes him by the ear as he starts screaming for Parpignol's toys. The mothers, weakening, buy the toys. Parpignol goes off, with the children following, making a great racket with the trumpets, drums and tambourines.)

RODOLFO
(sottovoce a Mimì)
(softly to Mimì)
E tu, Mimì, che vuoi?
And you, Mimì, what do you want?

MIMÌ
La crema.
The custard.

SCHAUNARD
(al cameriere)
(to the waiter)
E gran sfarzo. C'è una dama!
And great pomp. There is a lady!

RAGAZZI E BAMBINE
BOYS AND GIRLS
Viva Parpignol!
Long live Parpignol!

MARCELLO
(galantemente, a Mimì)
(gallantly, to Mimì)
Signorina Mimì, che dono raro
Miss Mimì, what gift rare

le ha fatto il suo Rodolfo?
you has made your Rodlfo?
(What rare gift has your Rodolfo given you?)

MIMÌ
Una cuffietta a pizzi tutta rosa ricamata;
A bonnet with lace all pink, embroidered;

coi miei capelli bruni ben si fonde.
with my hair brown well it goes.
(it goes well with my brown hair.)

Da tanto tempo tal cuffietta è cosa desiata!
For a long time such (a) bonnet is (a) thing wished!
(I've wanted such a bonnet for a long time!)

Ed egli ha letto quel che il core asconde...
And he has read that which my heart hides...
(And he has read in my heart my secret wish to have it.)

Ora colui che legge dentro a un cuore
Now he who reads inside in a heart
(Now, he who can read inside a person's heart)

sa l'amore...ed è lettore.
knows love...and is (a) reader.
(knows about love and is a very special reader.)

SCHAUNARD
Esperto professore...
Expert professor...

COLLINE
Che ha già diplomi
Who has already diplomas

e non son armi prime le sue rime.
and not are weapons new his rhymes.
(Who already has diplomas, and his rhymes are not beginner's weapons.)

SCHAUNARD
Tanto che sembra ver ciò che egli esprime!
So much so that seems true that which he expresses!
(So much so that what he expresses seems true!)

MARCELLO
(guardando Mimì)
(looking at Mimì)
O bella età d'inganni e d'utopie!
Oh beautiful age of deceits and utopias!

Si crede, spera, e tutto bello appare.
One believes, hopes, and all lovely seems.
(One believes and hopes, and all seems lovely.)

RODOLFO
La più divina delle poesie
The most divine of poems

è quella, amico, che c'insegna a amare!
is that one, friend, that teaches us to love!

MIMÌ
Amare è dolce ancora più del miele!
To love is sweeter even more than honey!

MARCELLO
Secondo il palato è miele o fiele!
According to one's taste, it's honey or gall!

MIMÌ
(sorpreso)
(surprised)

O Dio! L'ho offeso!
Oh God! I have him offended!
(Oh God! I've offended him!)

RODOLFO
È in lutto, o mia Mimì.
He's in mourning, oh my Mimì.

SCHAUNARD, COLLINE
(per cambiare discorso)
(to change the subject)
Allegri! E un *toast*.
Be happy! And a toast!

MARCELLO
Qua del liquor!
Here, some liquor!

MIMÌ, RODOLFO, MARCELLO
E via i pensier, alti i bicchier.
Away with the thoughts, high the glasses!

TUTTI
ALL
Beviam!
Let's drink!

MARCELLO
(vedendo Musetta che entra, ridendo:)
(having seen Musetta approaching, from afar, he interrupts shouting:)
Ch'io beva del tossico!
Let me drink some poison!

*(All'angolo di via Mazzarino appare una bellissima signora dal fare
civettuolo ed allegro, dal sorriso provocante. Le vien dietro un signore
pomposo, pieno di pretensione negli abiti, nei modi, nella persona.)*
*(A beautiful lady appears, with a flirtatious demeanor and provocative
smile. Behind her comes a pompous and affected old man. The lady, upon
seeing the friends' table, slows down. One could say that she has arrived at
the goal of her journey.)*

RODOLFO, SCHAUNARD, COLLINE
(con sorpresa, vedendo Musetta:)
(At Marcello's exclamation, they turn and exclaim:)
Oh!

MARCELLO
Essa!
She!

RODOLFO, SCHAUNARD, COLLINE
Musetta!

*(Gli amici, i loro occhi pieni di compassione, guardano Marcello, che
ha trasformato pallido. Il cameriere comincia a servire. Schaunard
e Colline guardano con discrezione verso Musetta e parlano di lei.
Marcello finge la massima indifferenza. Rodolfo notando nulla, ha
occhi solo per Mimì.)*
*(The friends, their eyes filled with compassion, look at Marcello, who has
turned pale. The waiter begins to serve. Schaunard and Colline look dis-
creetly towards Musetta and talk about her. Marcello feigns maximum
indifference. Rodolfo, noticing nothing, has eyes only for Mimì.)*

LE BOTTEGAIE
THE MOTHER SHOPKEEPERS
*(in piedi fuori i loro negozi a guardare Musetta, sussurrando tra
loro, puntando)*

(standing outside their shops to look at Musetta, whispering among themselves, pointing)
To'! Lei! Sì! Musetta! Siamo in auge! Che toeletta!
Well! She! Yes! Musetta! We're flourishing! What a get-up!

ALCINDORO
(trafelato)
(breathless, overtaking Musetta)
Come un facchino...
Like a porter...

correr di qua...di là...No! non ci sta...
running here...there...No! It isn't done!

MUSETTA
Vien, Lulù!
Come, Lulù!

ALCINDORO
Non ne posso più!
I can't stand any more!

SCHAUNARD
Quel brutto coso mi par che sudi!
That ugly thing methinks is sweating!
(I do believe that ugly thing is sweating!)

(Musetta vede la tavolata degli amici innanzi al Caffè Momus ed indica ad Alcindoro di sedersi al tavolo lasciato libero poco prima dai borghesi.)
(The beautiful lady, unmindful of the old man, goes towards the Café Momus and sits at a vacant table.)

ALCINDORO
Come? Qui fuori? Qui?
What! Here outside? Here?

MUSETTA
Siedi, Lulù.
Sit, Lulù.

(Siede irritato, alzando il bavero del suo pastrano e borbottando.)
(Alcindoro sits down, irritated, and turns up the collar of his coat.)

ALCINDORO
Tali nomignoli, prego, serbateli al tu per tu.[6]
Such pet names, please, save them for when we are alone!

(Un cameriere si avvicina e prepara la tavola.)
(A waiter has come over eagerly to prepare the table.)

MUSETTA
Non farmi il Barbablù!
Don't play the Bluebeard with me!

COLLINE
(esaminando il vecchio)
(examining the old man)
È il vizio contegnoso...
He is (the) vice sedate...
(Alcindoro is sedate vice personified...)

MARCELLO
(con disprezzo)
(with contempt)
Colla casta Susanna!
With the chaste Susanna!

MIMÌ
(a Rodolfo)
(to Rodolfo)
Essa è pur ben vestita.
She is yet well dressed!
(Yet, she is well dressed!)

RODOLFO
Gli angeli vanno nudi.
The angels go naked.[7]

MIMÌ
(curioso, a Rodolfo)
(curious, to Rodolfo)
La conosci? Chi è?
Her do you know? Who is she?

MARCELLO
Domandatelo a me.
Ask that to me.
(Ask *me* that!)

Il suo nome è Musetta; cognome: Tentazione!
Her name is Musetta; nickname: Temptation!

Per sua vocazione fa la rosa dei venti;
For her vocation (she) plays the rose of the winds;
(As her vocation she plays the compass needle;)

gira e muta soventi d'amanti e d'amore.
she turns and changes often lovers and (her) love.

E come la civetta,[8] è uccello sanguinario;
And like the owl, she's (a) bird sanguinary;
(And like the owl, she's a carnivorous bird…)

il suo cibo ordinario è il cuore!
her food usual is the heart!
(her usual food is the heart!)

Mangia il cuore!
She eats the heart!

Per questo io non ne ho più!
For that reason I not it have any longer!
(For that reason, I don't have a heart any longer!)

MUSETTA
(colpita nel vedere che gli amici non la guardano)
(struck at seeing that the friends do not look at her)
(Marcello mi vide…e non mi guarda il vile!
(Marcello me saw…and not me looks at, the coward!)
(Marcello saw me and the coward doesn't look at me!)

Quel Schaunard che ride! Mi fan tutti una bile!
That Schaunard who laughs! Me make all a bile!
(That Schaunard who laughs! They all gall me!)

Se potessi picchiar, se potessi graffiar!
If I could slap! If I could scratch!

Ma non ho sotto man che questo pelican!…Aspetta!)
But not have I at hand but this pelican!…Wait!)
(But all I have at hand is this pelican!…Wait!)

(Lei chiama il cameriere che era andato via.)
(She calls the waiter who had gone off.)

Ehi! Camerier!
Hey! Waiter!

MARCELLO
(nascondendo la commozione)
(to the friends, hiding the emotion that is overtaking him)
Passatemi il ragù!
Pass me the ragout!
(Pass me the stew!)

(Il cameriere accorre. Musetta prende un piatto e lo fiuta.)
(The waiter comes. Musetta takes a plate and smells it.)

MUSETTA
Ehi! Camerier! Questo piatto ha una puzza di rifritto!
Hey! Waiter! This plate has a smell of stale fat!

(Getta il piatto a terra con forza, il cameriere si affretta a raccogliere i cocci.)
(She throws the plate down and the waiter hastens to pick up the pieces.)

ALCINDORO
(cercando di calmarla)
(trying to calm her)
No! Musetta…Zitta, zitta!
No! Musetta!…Hush, hush!

MUSETTA
(vedendo che Marcello non si volta)
(angrily, still looking at Marcello)
(Ah! Non si volta! Ora lo batto!)
(Ah! Not he turns! Now him I'll hit!)
(Ah! He won't turn around! Now I'll hit him!)

ALCINDORO
Zitta! Modi, garbo! A chi parli?
Hush! Manners! Tact! To whom are you talking?

COLLINE
Questo pollo è un poema!
This chicken is a poem!

ALCINDORO
Conchi parli?
With whom are you speaking?

MUSETTA
(seccata)
(irked)
Al cameriere! Non seccar!
To the waiter! Don't bother me!

SCHAUNARD
Il vino è prelibato!
The wine is choice!

MUSETTA
Voglio fare il mio piacere...
I want to do my pleasure...
(I want to do what I please...)

ALCINDORO
Parla pian!
Speak softly!

MUSETTA
Vo' far quel che mi pare!
I want to do that which me suits!
(I want to do as I like!)

ALCINDORO
(Prende la nota del cameriere e si mette ad ordinare la cena.)
(He takes the menu from the waiter and begins to order dinner.)

Parla pian!
Speak softly!

MUSETTA
Non seccar!
Don't bother me!

SARTINE E STUDENTI
SEAMSTRESSES AND STUDENTS
(attraversando la scena)
(crossing the stage)
Guarda, guarda, chi si vede! Proprio lei, Musetta!
Look who is seen! Truly she, Musetta!
(Look who's there! It is Musetta all right!)

Con quel vecchio che balbetta, Ah! Ah! Ah!
With that old man who stammers, Ah! Ah! Ah!

MUSETTA
(Che sia geloso di questa mummia?)
(That he be jealous of this mummy?)
(Could he be jealous of this mummy?)

ALCINDORO
La convenienza...il grado...la virtù!
Propriety...rank...virtue!

MUSETTA
(fra se)
(aside)
Vediamo se mi resta
Let's see if (to) me remains

tanto poter su lui da farlo cedere!
so much power over him to make him give in!
(Let's see if I still have enough power over him to make him give in!)

SCHAUNARD
La commedia è stupenda!
The comedy is stupendous!

MUSETTA
(guardando Marcello a gran voce)
(looking at Marcello, in a loud voice)
Tu non mi guardi!
You not me look at!
(You aren't looking at me!)

ALCINDORO
Vedi bene che ordino!
You see clearly that I'm ordering!

SCHAUNARD
La commedia è stupenda!
The comedy is stupendous!

COLLINE
Stupenda!
Stupendous!

RODOLFO
(a Mimì)
(to Mimì)
Sappi per tuo governo
You should know for your guidance

che non darei perdono in sempiterno.

that not I would give pardon forever!

(that I wouldn't keep on forgiving you [if you ever behaved like that]!)

SCHAUNARD

(a Colline)

(to Colline)

Essa all'un parla

She to the one speaks

perché l'altro intenda.

so that the other one may understand.

(She speaks to the one, so that the other may understand.)

MIMÌ

(a Rodolfo)

(to Rodolfo)

Io t'amo tanto, e sono tutta tua…!

I love you so much and am all yours!

Che mi parli di perdono?

What (to) me you speak of forgiveness?

(Why do you speak to me of forgiveness?)

COLLINE

(a Schaunard)

(to Schaunard)

E l'altro invan crudel

And the other in vain cruel,

finge di non capir, ma sugge miel!
pretends of not understanding but sucks honey!
(The other one [Marcello], being cruel in vain, pretends not to
understand but sucks honey![9])

MUSETTA
Ma il tuo cuore martella!
But your heart is pounding!

ALCINDORO
Parla piano!
Speak softly!

MUSETTA
*(sempre seduta dirigendosi intenzionalmente a Marcello, il quale
comincia ad agitarsi)*
*(flirtatiously, turning with meaning towards Marcello, who begins to feel
uneasy)*
Quando men' vo soletta per la via
When I go along alone on the street

la gente sosta e mira,
the people stop and look,

e la bellezza mia
and the beauty mine

tutta ricerca in me, da capo a piè.
all seek in me from head to foot.
(the people seek all the beauty in me from head to foot.)

MARCELLO
(per gli amici)
(to the friends)

Legatemi alla seggiola!
Tie me to the chair!

ALCINDORO
Quella gente che dirà!
Those people what will they say!

MUSETTA
Ed assaporo allor la bramosia sottil
And I savor then the desire subtle

che dagli occhi traspira
that from the eyes breathes

e dai palesi vezzi intender sa
and from my obvious charms (to) appreciate knows

alle occulte beltà.
the hidden beauties.
(And I then savor the subtle desire that breathes forth from their eyes, which know how to appreciate the hidden beauties of my obvious charms.)

Cosi l'effluvio del desio tutta m'aggira,
Thus the flow of desire all of me surrounds,

felice mi fa!
happy me makes!
(it makes me happy!)

ALCINDORO
Quel canto scurrile mi muove la bile!
That song scurrilous me stirs the bile!
(That scurrilous song arouses my wrath!)

MUSETTA
E tu che sai, che memori e ti struggi…
And you who know, who remember and destroy yourself…

da me tanto rifuggi?
from me so you flee?

So ben: le angoscie tue non le vuoi dir,
I know well: the sufferings yours not them you wish to tell
(I know well that you don't wish to confess your suffering)

ma ti senti morir.
but you feel (yourself) dying!

MIMÌ
Io vedo ben che quella poveretta
I see well that that poor girl

tutta invaghita di Marcello ell'è!
all infatuated she is with Marcello!
(I can well see that that poor girl is all infatuated with Marcello.)

ALCINDORO
Quella gente che dirà!
These people what will they say!

RODOLFO
(a Mimì)
(to Mimì)
Marcello un dì l'amò, la fraschetta l'abbandonò
Marcello one day loved her, the coquette abandoned (him)

per poi darsi a miglior vita.
to then devote herself to (a) better life.

SCHAUNARD
Ah! Marcello cederà!
Ah! Marcello will give in!

COLLINE
Chi sa mai quel che avverrà!
Who knows ever what will happen!
(Who knows what will ever happen!)

SCHAUNARD
(Trovan dolce a pari il laccio...)
(They find sweet equally the noose...)

COLLINE
Santi numi, in simil briga...
Santi numi, in such a fix...

SCHAUNARD
(...chi lo tende e chi ci dà.)
(...who it extends and who is trapped in it.)
(They find the noose equally sweet...the one who sets it and the
one who is trapped in it.)

COLLINE
...mai Colline intopperà!
...never Colline will fall into!
(Colline will never fall into such a situation!)

MUSETTA
(Ah! Marcello smania, Marcello è vinto!)
(Ah! Marcello is raving! Marcello is defeated!)

MIMÌ
(Quell'infelice mi muove a pietà.)
(That unhappy woman me moves to pity.)

ALCINDORO
Parla piano! Zitta!
Speak softly! Hush!

COLLINE
(Essa è bella, io non son cieco…)
(She is lovely, I not am blind…)

MIMÌ
(a Rodolfo)
(to Rodolfo)
T'amo!
I love you!

RODOLFO
Mimì!

SCHAUNARD
(Quel bravaccio a momenti cederà!
(That swaggerer any moment will give in!)

Stupenda è la commedia! Marcello cederà.)
Stupendous is the comedy! Marcello will give in!)

(a Colline)
(to Colline)

Se una tal vaga persona ti trattasse a tu per tu
If such (a) lovely person to you spoke intimately

la tua scienza brontolona manderesti a Belzebù.
your science grumpy you'd send to Beelzebub!
(If such a lovely lady were to speak intimately with you, you'd send
your grumpy science to Hell!)

MUSETTA
(verso Marcello)
(towards Marcello)
So ben: le angoscie tue non le vuoi dir.
I know well: the sufferings yours not them you wish to tell.
(I know well that you don't wish to confess your sufferings.)

Ah! ma ti senti morir!
Ah! But you feel (yourself) dying!

(ad Alcindoro)
(to Alcindoro)

Io voglio fare il mio piacere,
I want to do my pleasure!
(I want to do as I please!)

Voglio far quel che mi par! Non seccar!
I want to do what suits me! Don't bother me!

MIMÌ
Quell'infelice mi muove a pietà.
That unhappy girl me moves to pity!

L'amor ingeneroso è tristo amor!
Love ungenerous is sad love!
(Ungenerous love is a sad kind of love.)

RODOLFO
È fiacco amor quell che le offese vendicar non sa!
It's a weak love that which the offenses avenge not can!
(Love which cannot avenge its insults is a weak kind of love.)

Non risorge spento amor!
Not rises again dead love!
(Dead love does not return.)

COLLINE
Ma piaccionmi assai più una pipa e un testo greco.
But pleases me much more a pipe and a text Greek.
(But I'm pleased much more by a pipe and a Greek text.)

Essa è bella, non son cieco, *ecc.*
She is lovely, I am not blind!

ALCINDORO
Modi! Garbo! Zitta!
Manners! Tact! Hush!

MUSETTA
Non seccar! Or conviene liberarsi del vecchio!
Don't bother me! Now it's best to liberate oneself from the old man!

(*fingendo un dolore*)
(*pretending to feel a sharp pain*)

Ahi!
Ouch!

ALCINDORO
Che c'è?
What is it?

MUSETTA
Qual dolore! Qual bruciore!
What pain! What burning!

ALCINDORO
Dove?
Where?

MUSETTA
Al piè! Sciogli, slaccia! Rompi, straccia, te ne imploro!
In my foot! Loosen, unlace! Break, tear, I implore you!

Laggiù c'è un calzolaio.
Down there there's a shoemaker.

Corri, presto! Ne voglio un altro paio!
Run, quickly! Of them I want another pair!

Ahi! che fitta, maledetta scarpa stretta! Or la levo.
Ouch! What pain! Cursed shoe narrow! Now I'll take it off.

Eccola qua. Corri, va, presto!
Here it is. Run, go, quickly!

MARCELLO
(commosso sommamente, avanzandosi)
(greatly moved)
Gioventù mia, tu non sei morta
Youth mine, you not are dead

né di te è morto il sovvenir!
nor of you dead is the memory!
(My youth, you're not dead and neither is the memory of you!)

Se tu battessi alla mia porta
If you knocked at my door

t'andrebbe il mio core ad aprir!
would go my heart to open!
(My heart would go to open the door if you knocked at it.)

ALCINDORO
Imprudente! Quella gente che dirà?
Imprudent one! Those people what will they say?

Ma il mio grado! Vuoi ch'io comprometta? Aspetta!
But my rank! Do you want me compromised? Wait!

(Nasconde prontamente nel gilet la scarpa di Musetta, poi si abbottona l'abito. Alcindoro va via frettolosamente.)
(He desperately takes the shoe and quickly stuffs it into his vest. He then buttons his coat majestically and for fear of further scandal, runs hastily towards the cobbler's shop.)

Musetta, vo!
Musetta, I'm going!

SCHAUNARD, COLLINE
(La commedia è stupenda!)
(The comedy is stupendous!)

RODOLFO
(Io vedo ben: la commedia è stupenda!)
(I see well: the comedy is stupendous!)

MIMÌ
(Io vedo ben: ell'è invaghita di Marcello!)
(I see well: she is infatuated with Marcello!)

MUSETTA
Marcello!

MARCELLO
Sirena!
Siren!

SCHAUNARD
Siamo all'ultima scena!
We're at the last scene!

(Il cameriere porta un conto.)
(A waiter brings the bill.)

RODOLFO, COLLINE, SCHAUNARD
Il conto?!
The bill?!

SCHAUNARD
Così presto?
So soon?

COLLINE
Chi l'ha richiesto?
Who has asked for it?

SCHAUNARD
Vediam!
Let's see!

(Dopo guardato il conto, lo passa agli amici.)
(He takes the bill, which then makes the rounds of all the friends.)

RODOLFO, COLLINE
Caro!
Expensive!

RODOLFO, SCHAUNARD, COLLINE
Fuori il danaro!
Out (with) the money!

SCHAUNARD
Colline, Rodolfo, e tu, Marcel?
Colline, Rodolfo, and you, Marcello?

MARCELLO
Sono all'asciutto!
We're broke!

SCHAUNARD
Come?
What?

RODOLFO
Ho trenta soldi in tutto!
I've thirty *sous* in all!

MARCELLO, SCHAUNARD, COLLINE
Come? Non ce n'è più?
What? Not there is more?
(What! There isn't any more?)

SCHAUNARD
(terribile)
(in terror)
Ma il mio tesoro ov'è?
But my treasure where is it?

(Portano le mani alle tasche: sono vuote: nessuno sa spiegarsi la rapida scomparsa degli scudi di Schaunard sorpresi si guardano l'un l'altro. Si ode avvicinarsi un suon di tamburi.)

(They put their hands in their pockets and find them empty. Nobody can explain the rapid disappearance of Schaunard's money. Surprised, they look at each other. In the meanwhile from far off is heard the approaching military tattoo. The people run in from all sides, looking and running to and fro, to see from which direction it is coming.)

MONELLI E BOURGEOIS, SARTINE E STUDENTI
URCHINS AND BOURGEOIS, SEAMSTRESSES AND STUDENTS
La ritirata!
The tattoo!

MONELLI
URCHINS
S'avvicinan per di qua?
Are they getting closer along here?

MUSETTA
(al cameriere)
(to the waiter)
Il mio conto date a me.
My bill give (it) to me.

SARTINE, STUDENTI
SEAMSTRESSES, STUDENTS
No! Di là! S'avvicinan per di là!
It's coming from here! No! It's coming from there!

MUSETTA
(al cameriere che le mostra il conto)
(to the waiter, who hands her the bill)
Bene!
Very well!

BORGHESI, VENDITORI
BOURGEOIS, VENDORS
Largo!
Make way!

ALCUNI BAMBINI
SOME CHILDREN
(dalle finestre)
(from windows)
Voglio veder! Voglio sentir!
I want to see! I want to hear!

MUSETTA
(al cameriere)
(to the waiter)
Presto sommate quello con questo!
Quickly add up that with this!

MAMME
MOTHERS
Lisetta, vuoi tacere? Tonio, la vuoi finire?
Lisetta, will you be quiet? Tonio, you will it stop!

ALCUNI BAMBINI
SOME CHILDREN
Mamma, voglio vedere! Papà, voglio sentire!
Mamma, I want to see! Daddy, I want to hear!

MUSETTA
Paga il signor che stava qui con me.
Pays the gentleman who was here with me!
(The gentleman who was here with me will pay.)

RODOLFO, SCHAUNARD, COLLINE, MARCELLO
Paga il signor!
Pays the gentleman!
(The gentleman will pay!)

LA FOLLA
THE CROWD
S'avvicinano di qua! Sì, di qua!
They're nearing from here! Yes, from here!

MONELLI
URCHINS
Come sarà arrivata la seguiremo al passo!
As soon as it arrives it we'll follow at pace!
(As soon as the parade arrives, we'll follow it at its pace.)

MUSETTA
(ponendo i due bollette, sommati insieme, a casa di Alcindoro)
(placing the two bills, added together, at Alcindoro's place)
E dove s'è seduto, ritrovi il mio saluto!
And where he'd been sitting may he find my farewell!

BORGHESI
BOURGEOIS
In quel rullio tu senti la patria maestà!
In that drumroll you feel the nation's majesty!

RODOLFO, MARCELLO, SCHAUNARD, COLLINE
E dove s'è seduto ritrovi il suo saluto!
And where he'd been sitting may he find her farewell!

LA FOLLA
THE CROWD
Largo! Eccoli qua! In fila!
Make way! Here they are! Line up!

MONELLI
URCHINS
Ohè! Attenti! Eccoli qua! In fila!
Hey! Watch! Here they are! Line up!

MARCELLO, RODOLFO, COLLINE
Giunge la Ritirata!
Here comes the tattoo!

Che il vecchio non ci veda fuggir colla sua preda!
That the old man not us see run away with his prey!
(The old man shouldn't see us running away with his prey!)

MARCELLO, SCHAUNARD, COLLINE
Quella folla serrata il nascondiglio appresti!
That crowd packed the hiding place will provide!
(Let's hide in that packed crowd!)

(Il tatuaggio militare attraversa la scena.)
(The military tattoo crosses the stage.)

LA FOLLA
THE CROWD
Ecco il tambur maggiore!
Here is the drum major!

Più fiero d'un antico guerrier!
More proud than an ancient warrior!

TUTTI GLI AMICI, PLUS MIMÌ E MUSETTA
ALL THE FRIENDS, PLUS MIMÌ AND MUSETTA
Lesti! Lesti!
Quickly! Quickly!

LA FOLLA
THE CROWD
I Zappator, olà! Ecco il tambur maggior!
The Sappers, hey! Here's the drum major!

Pare un general! La Ritirata è qua!
He looks like a general! The tattoo is here!

Eccola là, il bel tambur maggior!
There he is, the handsome drum major!

La canna d'or, tutto splendor!
The baton of gold, all splendor!

Che guarda, passa, va!
Who looks, passes, goes on!

Di Francia è il più bell'uom!
Of France he is the most handsome man!
(He is the most handsome man in France!)

RODOLFO, COLLINE, SCHAUNARD, MARCELLO
Viva Musetta! Cuor biricchin!
Long live Musetta! Heart roguish!
(Long live Musetta of the roguish heart!)

Gloria ed onor, onor e Gloria del Quartier Latin!
Glory and honor of the Latin Quarter!

(Musetta non potendo camminare con una scarpa sola, è alzata a braccia di Marcello e Colline. Tutti si mettono in coda alla ritirata e si allontanano. Alcindoro torna con un paio di scarpe; il cameriere gli presenta i conti. Vedendo la somma e non trovando più nessuno, Alcindoro cade su di una sedia, stupefatto.)

(Because Musetta has only one shoe she cannot walk and is lifted up and carried by Marcello and Colline. The crowd, seeing Musetta carried triumphantly, uses this as a pretext to give her a noisy ovation. Marcello and Colline with Musetta take up the rear of the tattoo. Rodolfo and Mimì, arm in arm, follow them, along with Schaunard with his horn to his lips. Everyone follows the parade. Alcindoro returns, with a pair of well-wrapped shoes, and looks in vain for Musetta. He goes to the table and the waiter who is near it ceremoniously presents him with the bills left by Musetta. Alcindoro sees the sum and falls aghast and amazed in the chair.)

FINE DI ATTO II
END OF ACT II

ATTO TERZO
ACT III

La Barriera d'Enfer
The Barrière d'Enfer

(Al di là della barriera il boulevard esterno, a sinistra un cabaret e un piccolo largo costeggiato da alcuni platani. Certi doganieri dormono avanti ad un braciere. Dal cabaret, ad intervalli, grida, risate. È un'alba di febbraio. La neve è dappertutto. Dietro la cancellata chiusa, battendo i piedi dal freddo, stanno alcuni spazzini.)
(Beyond the tollgate on the boulevard outside Paris, and, in the far background the Orleans Road which disappears amid the tall houses in the February fog. To one side is a tavern, which uses Marcello's painting of the "Crossing of the Red Sea" as its sign. It is early dawn and there is snow everywhere. The customs men are dozing seated before a brazier. From the tavern, at intervals, one hears shouts, clinking of glasses and laughter. A customs man comes from the tavern with some wine. Beyond the closed tollgate, stamping their feet with the cold and blowing on their frozen hands, are some street sweepers.)

SPAZZINI
SWEEPERS
Ohè, là, le guardie! Aprite!
Hey there, (the) guards! Open!

Quelli di Gentilly! Siam gli spazzini!
Those of Gentilly! We're the sweepers!
(Hey there! Guards! Open up! We're the sweepers from Gentilly!)

Fiocca la neve…Ohè, là! Qui s'agghiaccia!
Is falling the snow…Hey there! Here one freezes!
(It's snowing…Hey there! We're freezing!)

(Gli uomini doganali cominciano a muoversi.)
(The customs men begin to stir.)

UN DOGANIERE
A CUSTOMS MAN
Vengo!
I'm coming!

(Va ad aprire, gli Spazzini entrano e si allontanano per la via d'Enfer.
Il Doganiere richiude la cancellata.)
(He goes and opens the gate. Afterwards the sweepers enter and then go off
by the Rue d'Enfer. The customs man shuts the gate again. From the tavern
merry singing is heard accompanied by the sound of happy voices and the
clinking of glasses.)

VOCI DAL CABARET
VOICES WITHIN
Chi nel ber trovò il piacer
Who in drinking found pleasure

nel suo bicchier, Ah!
in his glass, ah!
(Whoever has found pleasure in his glass)

d'una bocca nell'ardor trovò l'amor!
of a mouth in the ardor found love!
(has found love in the ardor of a mouth!)

MUSETTA
(da dentro la taverna)
(from inside the tavern)
Ah! Se nel bicchier sta il piacer,
Ah! If in the glass is the pleasure,

in giovin bocca sta l'amor.
in young mouth is love!
(Ah! If pleasure is found in the glass, love is found in a young mouth!)

VOCI DAL CABARET
VOICES WITHIN
Trallerallè. Eva e Noè!
Fa-la-la-la, Eve and Noah!

(Suoni di carrettieri sono sentito passando con i loro carri e screpo-
lature le fruste.)
(Sounds of carters are heard passing by with their wagons and cracking
their whips.)

CARRETTIERI E LATTIVENDOLE
CARTERS AND MILKWOMEN
Hopp-là!
Giddyap!

DOGANIERE
A CUSTOMS MAN
Son già le lattivendole!
It's already the milkwomen!
(The milkwomen are here already!)

(Egli apre il cancello. Una fila di carretti con contadini entra assieme alle lattaie.)
(The customs sergeant comes out of the guard house and orders the gate to be opened. The milkwomen pass through on their donkeys and go off in several directions.)

CARRETTIERI E LATTIVENDOLE
CARTERS AND MILKWOMEN
Hopp-là!
Giddyap!

LE LATTIVENDOLE
MILKWOMEN
Buon giorno!
Good day!

LE CONTADINE
PEASANT WOMEN
(entering the scene with baskets arm)
(with baskets on their arms)
Burro e cacio! Polli ed ova!
Butter and cheese! Chickens and eggs!

(I Doganieri le lasciano passare.)
(They pay and the customs man lets them through.)

Voi da che parte andate?
You, which way are you going?

A San Michele! Ci troverem più tardi?
To Saint Michael! Shall we meet later?

A mezzodì!
At noon!

(Si allontanano. Entra Mimì. Appena giunta al primo platano la coglie un accesso di tosse. Poi riavutasi dice al sergente:)
(They go off in several directions. The customs men take away the benches and the brazier. Mimì comes in looking around carefully, trying to recognize the place, and is seized by a fit of coughing as she reaches the first tree. When she recovers, she goes to the sergeant.)

MIMÌ
(al Sergente)
(to the sergeant)
Sa dirmi, scusi, qual è l'osteria dove un pittor lavora?
Can you tell me, excuse me, where is the tavern where a painter works?

SERGENTE
SERGEANT
(indicando il Cabaret)
(indicating the tavern)
Eccola!
There it is!

MIMÌ
Grazie!
Thank you!

(Esce la fantesca dal cabaret. Mimì le si avvicina.)
(A maidservant comes out from the tavern. Mimì goes near her.)

O buona donna, mi fate il favore...
Oh good woman, me do the favor...
(Oh good woman, do me the favor...)

di cercarmi il pittore Marcello?
of finding me the painter Marcello?

Ho da parlargli. Ho tanta fretta.
I have to speak to him. I'm in such a hurry.

Ditegli, piano, che Mimì l'aspetta.
Tell him softly that Mimì is waiting for him.

SERGENTE
SERGEANT
(ad uno che passa)
(to a passing man)
Ehi! Quel paniere!
Hey! That basket!

DOGANIERE
CUSTOMS MAN
Vuoto!
Empty!

SERGENTE
SERGEANT
Passi!
Let him pass.

(Dalla barriera entra altra gente, e chi da una parte, chi dall'altra tutti si allontanano. Le campane dell'ospizio Maria Teresa suonano mattutino. È giorno fatto, giorno d'inverno, triste e caliginoso. Dal Cabaret escono alcune coppie che rincasano.)
(It is daylight now, a sad and snowy winter day. Some couples leave the tavern on their way home. Marcello comes out of the tavern and sees Mimì.)

MARCELLO
Mimì?!

MIMÌ
Speravo di trovarvi qui.
I was hoping to find you here.

MARCELLO
È ver, siam qui da un mese di quell'oste alle spese.
It's true, we're here since a month at that tavern keeper's expense.

Musetta insegna il canto ai passeggieri
Musetta teaches singing to the travellers,

Io pingo quei guerrieri sulla facciata.
I paint those warriors on the façade.

(Mimì tossisce.)
(Mimì coughs.)

È freddo. Entrate.
It's cold. Come in.

MIMÌ
C'è Rodolfo?
There's Rodolfo?
(Is Rodolfo there?)

MARCELLO
Sì.
Yes.

MIMÌ
Non posso entrar, no, no!
Not can I go in, no, no!

MARCELLO
(sorpreso)
(surprised)
Perché?
Why?

MIMÌ
(scoppia in pianto)
(busting out in tears)
O buon Marcello, aiuto!
Oh good Marcello, help!

MARCELLO
Cos'è avvenuto?
What has happened?

MIMÌ
Rodolfo m'ama e mi fugge,
Rodolfo loves me and (from) me flees,

il mio Rodolfo si strugge per gelosia.
my Rodolfo himself (is) consumed by jealousy.

Un passo, un detto, un vezzo, un fior…
A footstep, a word, a compliment, a flower…

lo mettono in sospetto…
him put in suspicion…
(arouse his suspicion…)

onde corrucci ed ire.
whereupon, frowns and anger.

Talor la notte fingo di dormire
At times at night I pretend to sleep

e in me lo sento fiso
and in me him I feel staring,

spiarmi i sogni in viso.
spying the dreams on (my) face.
(and inside myself I feel him looking at my face and spying on my dreams.)

Mi grida ad ogni istante: Non fai per me,
At me he shouts at every moment: You're not for me,

ti prendi un altro amante, non fai per me! Ahimè!
get yourself another lover, you're not for me! Alas!

In lui parla il rovello, lo so,
In him speaks the anger, I know it
(I know it's his anger speaking)

ma che rispondergli, Marcello?
but what (to) answer him, Marcello?
(but what can I answer him, Marcello?)

MARCELLO
Quando s'è come voi non si vive in compagnia.
When one is like you, one doesn't live together.
(When people are like you two, they don't live together.)

MIMÌ
Dite bene, lasciarci conviene.
You say right, you say right, to part from each other is best.

Aiutateci, aiutateci voi!
Help us, help us, you!

noi s'è provato più volte, ma invano.
we have tried many times, but in vain.

MARCELLO
Son lieve a Musetta, ella è lieve a me,
I'm easy with Musetta, she's easy with me,

perché ci amiamo in allegria…
because we love each other in happiness…

Canti e risa, ecco il fior d'invariabile amor!
Songs and laughter, there's the flower of unchanging love!

MIMÌ
Dite bene, lasciarci conviene!
You're right, to leave each other is best!

Fate voi per il meglio.
Do you for the best.
(You do what is best.)

MARCELLO
Sta ben! Ora lo sveglio.
All right! Now him I will wake.
(All right! I will wake him now.)

MIMÌ
Dorme?
Is he asleep?

MARCELLO
È piombato qui un'ora avanti l'alba,
He rushed in here an hour before dawn,

s'assopì sopra una panca. Guardate.
he dozed off on a bench. Look.

(Fa cenno a Mimì di guardare per la finestra dentro il Cabaret. Mimì tossisce.)
(He goes near the window and motions to Mimì to look. Mimì coughs.)

Che tosse!
What a cough!

MIMÌ
Da ieri ho l'ossa rotte.[1]
Since yesterday I have bones broken.

Fuggì da me stanotte dicendomi:
He fled from me last night saying to me:

È finita. A giorno sono uscita
"It's finished." At daybreak I went out

e me ne venni a questa volta.
and I came in this direction.

MARCELLO
(osservando Rodolfo nell'interno)
(observing Rodolfo inside the tavern)
Si desta…s'alza…mi cerca…viene…
He's awakening…he's rising…he's looking for me…he's coming…

MIMÌ
Ch'ei non mi veda.
He shouldn't see me!

MARCELLO
Or rincasate, Mimì, per carità! Non fate scene qua!
Now go home, Mimì, for pity's sake! Don't make scenes here!

(Mimì si nasconde dietro un platano. Rodolfo accorre dal cabaret.)
(He pushes Mimì gently towards the corner of the tavern, but almost imme-diately, she extends her head out, curious. Marcello runs towards Rodolfo.)

RODOLFO
(esce dal Cabaret ed accorre verso Marcello)
(running towards Marcello)
Marcello, finalmente! Qui niun ci sente.
Marcello, finally! Here no one us hears.

Io voglio separarmi da Mimì!
I want to separate from Mimì!

MARCELLO
Sei volubil cosi?
Are you fickle like that?

RODOLFO
Già un'altra volta credetti morto il mio cor,
Already another time I believed dead my heart,
(Already once before I believed that my heart was dead,)

ma di quegli occhi azzurri allo splendor
but of those eyes blue at the glow
(but at the glow of those blue eyes)

esso è risorto. Ora il tedio l'assale…
it has revived. Now (the) boredom assails it…

MARCELLO
E gli vuoi rinnovare il funeral?
And to it you want to repeat the funeral?
(And you want to repeat your heart's funeral?)

RODOLFO
(con dolore)
(with pain)
Per sempre!
For ever!

MARCELLO
Cambia metro.
Change your tune.

Dei pazzi è l'amor tetro
Of madmen is love gloomy

che lacrime distilla.
that tears distills.
(Gloomy love that causes tears to flow belongs to madmen.)

Se non ride e sfavilla,
If it doesn't laugh and sparkle

l'amore è fiacco e roco.
love is weak and hoarse.

Tu sei geloso.
You are jealous.

RODOLFO
Un poco.
A little.

MARCELLO
Collerico, lunatico, imbevuto di pregiudizi, noioso, cocciuto!
Choleric, lunatic, steeped in prejudices, bothersome, stubborn!

MIMÌ
(fra sé, a disagio)
(to herself, uneasily)
(Or lo fa incollerire! Me poveretta!)
(Now him he'll make angry! Me poor one!)
(Poor me! Now he's going to make him angry.)

RODOLFO
Mimì è una civetta che frascheggia con tutti.
Mimì is a coquette who flirts with everyone.

Un moscardino di Viscontino le fa l'occhio di triglia.
A little dandy of (a) Viscount at her makes eyes of mullet.
(A little dandy of a Viscount makes fish eyes at her.)

Ella sgonnella e scopre la caviglia
She wiggles and bares her ankle

con un far promettente e lusinghier…
with a manner promising and flattering…

MARCELLO
Lo devo dir? Non mi sembri sincer.
It must I say? Not to me you seem sincere.
(I must say that you don't seem sincere to me.)

RODOLFO
Ebbene, no, non lo son.
All right no, not it I am.
(All right, no, I'm not sincere.)

Invan nascondo la mia vera tortura.
In vain I hide my true torment.

Amo Mimì sovra ogni cosa al mondo,
I love Mimì above every thing in the world,

io l'amo, ma ho paura.
I love her, but I'm afraid.

(Mimì, sorpreso, arriva ancora di più, sempre nascosto dietro gli
alberi.)
(Mimì, surprised, comes still closer, always hidden behind the trees.)

Mimì è tanto malata! Ogni di più declina.
Mimì is so sick! Every day further she worsens.

La povera piccina è condannata!
The poor little girl is doomed!

MARCELLO
Mimì?

MIMÌ
Che vuol dire?
What does he mean?

RODOLFO
Una terribil tosse l'esil petto le scuote...
A terrible cough the fragile chest her racks...
(A terrible cough racks her fragile chest,)

già le smunte gote di sangue ha rosse...
already the emaciated cheeks of blood she has red...
(already her emaciated cheeks are flushed.)

MARCELLO
Povera Mimì!
Poor Mimì!

MIMÌ
Ahimè, morire?
Alas, to die?!

RODOLFO
La mia stanza è una tana squallida...
My room is a den squalid...
(My room is a squalid den...)

Il fuoco è spento.
The fire I've put out.

V'entra e l'aggira il vento di tramontana.
There enters and moves about the wind of beyond the mountains.
(I've had to let the fire go out and the north wind enters into my
squalid room and blows about.)

Essa canta e sorride, e il rimorso m'assale.
She sings and smiles, and (the) remorse assails me.

Me, cagion del fatale mal che l'uccide.
I (the) cause of the fatal disease that is killing her.

MARCELLO
Che far dunque?
What to do then?

MIMÌ
(angosciato)
(anguished)
O mia vita!
Oh, my life!

RODOLFO
Mimì di serra è fiore. Povertà l'ha sfiorita;
Mimì of hothouse is (a) flower. Poverty has her blighted;
(Mimì is a hothouse flower, poverty has blighted her,)

per richiamarla in vita non basta amore!
in order to call her back to life not enough is love!
(in order to restore her health and bring her back to life, love is
not enough!)

MIMÌ
Ahimè! È finita! O mia vita....ahimè, morir!
Alas! It's finished! Oh my life...alas, to die!

MARCELLO
Oh qual pieta! Poveretta! Povera Mimì!
Oh what pity! Poor girl! Poor Mimì!

(Mimì singhiozza e tossisce.)
(Mimì's violent coughing and sobbing reveal her presence.)

RODOLFO
(vedendola e accorrendo a lei)
(seeing her and running to her)

Che! Mimì! Tu qui? M'hai sentito?
What? Mimì! You here? You have heard me?

MARCELLO
Ella dunque ascoltava?
She then was listening?

RODOLFO
(cercando di fare luce di ciò che Mimì si è sentito)
(trying to make light of what Mimì has overheard)
Facile alla paura, per nulla io m'arrovello.
Easily frightened, over nothing I get angry.

Vien là nel tepore!
Come there in the warmth!

(Vuol farla entrare nel cabaret.)
(He urges her to enter the tavern.)

MIMÌ
No, quel tanfo mi soffoca!
No, that moldy smell me chokes!
(No, that moldy smell in there chokes me!)

RODOLFO
Ah! Mimì!

(Stringe amorosamente Mimì fra le sue braccia e l'accarezza. Dal Cabaret si ode ridere sfacciatamente Musetta.)
(Rodolfo lovingly clasps Mimì in his arms. Musetta is heard laughing shamelessly from the tavern. Marcello runs to the window of the tavern.)

MARCELLO
È Musetta che ride. Con chi ride?
It's Musetta that's laughing. With whom is she laughing?

Ah la civetta! Imparerai!
Ah the coquette! You will learn!
(Ah! You flirt, I'll teach you!)

MIMÌ
(svincolandosi da Rodolfo)
(freeing herself from Rodolfo)
Addio.
Good-bye!

RODOLFO
Che! Vai?
What! You're going?

MIMÌ
D'onde lieta usci al tuo grido d'amore,
From where happily (she) left at your call of love,

torna sola Mimì al solitario nido
returns alone Mimì to the lonely nest.
(Mimì will now return to her lonely nest, which she once happily
left when she heard your call of love.)

Ritorna un'altra volta a intesser finti fior!
She returns once again to weave false flowers!

Addio, senza rancor.
Good-bye without bitterness.

Ascolta, le poche robe aduna che lasciai sparse.
Listen, the few things gather which I left scattered.
(Listen, gather the few things that I left scattered.)

Nel mio cassetto stan chiusi quel cerchietto d'or
In my drawer are shut that ring of gold
(I have shut away the gold ring in my drawer)

e il libro di preghiere.
and the book of prayers.

Involgi tutto quanto in un grembiale
Wrap everything in an apron

e manderò il portiere...
and I will send the concierge...

Bada, sotto il guanciale c'è la cuffietta rosa.
Mind you, under the pillow there is the bonnet pink.

Se vuoi serbarla a ricordo d'amor!
If you wish to keep it as a memory of love...

Addio senza rancor.
Good-bye without bitterness.

RODOLFO
Dunque è proprio finita!
Then it's really finished!

Te ne vai, la mia piccina? Addio, sogni d'amor!
You're leaving, my little one? Good-bye, dreams of love!

MIMÌ
Addio, dolce svegliare alla mattina!
Good-bye, sweet awakening in the morning!

RODOLFO
Addio, sognante vita…
Good-bye, dreaming life…
(Good-bye, life of dreams.)

MIMÌ
(sorridendo)
(smiling)
Addio, rabbuffi e gelosie…
Good-bye, rebukes and jealousies…

RODOLFO
che un tuo sorriso acqueta.
which one of your smiles calms.

MIMÌ
Addio, sospetti…
Good-bye, suspicions…

RODOLFO
Baci…
Kisses…

MIMÌ
…pungenti amarezze!
…poignant bitternesses!

RODOLFO
Ch'io da vero poeta rimavo con carezze!
Which I as a true poet rhymed with: caresses!

MIMÌ, RODOLFO
Soli l'inverno è cosa da morire.
Alone in winter is (a) thing to die of!

MIMÌ
Soli!
Alone!

MIMÌ, RODOLFO
Mentre a primavera c'è compagno il sol.
While in spring, there is companion the sun!
(While in spring, there is the sun for a companion!)

(Marcello e Musetta escono, bisticciando.)
(From the tavern is heard the noise of broken glasses and plates. The excited voices of Marcello and Musetta are heard.)

MARCELLO
Che facevi? Che dicevi…?
What were you doing? What were you saying…?

MUSETTA
Che vuoi dir?
What do you mean?

MARCELLO
Presso il foco a quel signore?
Near the fire, to that gentleman?

MUSETTA
Che vuoi dir?
What do you mean?

MIMÌ
Niuno è solo l'april...
No one is alone in April...

(Musetta esce con rabbia. Marcello la segue, fermandosi davanti alla porta.)
(Musetta comes out angrily. Marcello follows her, stopping at the door.)

MARCELLO
Al mio venire hai mutato di colore.
At my coming you changed (of) color.

MUSETTA
Quel signore mi diceva: "Ama il ballo, signorina?"
That gentleman to me was saying: "Do you like dancing, Miss?"

MARCELLO
Vana, frivola civetta!
Vain, frivolous flirt!

RODOLFO
Si parla coi gigli e le rose...
One speaks with the lilies and the roses...

MIMÌ
Esce dai nidi un cinguettio gentile.
Comes out from the nests a twittering gentle.
(A gentle twittering comes out of the nests.)

MUSETTA
Arrossendo io rispondevo: "Ballerei sera e mattina..."
Blushing I answered: "I would dance night and day..."

MARCELLO
Quel discorso asconde mire disoneste...
That talk hides intentions dishonest!
(Your talk hides dishonest intentions...!)

MUSETTA
Voglio piena libertà!
I want full freedom!

MARCELLO
(quasi avventandosi contro Musetta)
(almost hurling himself against Musetta)
Io t'acconcio per le feste² se ti colgo a incivettire!
I'll give you a severe thrashing if you I catch at flirting!

MUSETTA
Che mi canti?
What to me are you singing?
(What's this tune of yours?)

MIMÌ, RODOLFO
Al fiorir di primavera c'è compagno il sol!
At the flowering of spring, there's companion the sun!
(At the flowering of spring we have the sun for companion.)

MUSETTA
Che mi gridi, che mi canti?
What at me are you shouting? What at me are you singing?
(What are you shouting at me? What tune are you singing to me?)

All'altar non siamo uniti.
At the altar we're not joined!

Jan Peerce as Rodolfo, 1946
METROPOLITAN OPERA ARCHIVES

Giuseppe Di Stefano as Rodolfo, 1949

Richard Tucker as Rodolfo, 1949

Richard Tucker as Rodolfo, 1949
METROPOLITAN OPERA ARCHIVES

Set design for Act I by Joseph Novak, 1951
METROPOLITAN OPERA ARCHIVES

Giuseppe Valdengo as Marcello and Bidú Sayão as Mimì, 1951
METROPOLITAN OPERA ARCHIVES

Design sketches for the 1952 production by Rolf Gérard
METROPOLITAN OPERA ARCHIVES

Renata Tebaldi as Mimì, 1957

Mirella Freni as Mimì, 1965

Renata Scotto as Mimì and Luciano Pavarotti as Rodolfo, 1976
METROPOLITAN OPERA ARCHIVES

Teresa Stratas as Mimì and José Carreras as Rodolfo, 1981
METROPOLITAN OPERA ARCHIVES

Bohème – atto III –   Zeffirelli   3 Nov 1980

Set designs by Franco Zeffirelli, 1981

A scene from Act II of Franco Zeffirelli's 2006 production
Ken Howard/Metropolitan Opera

Rolando Villazón as Rodolfo, 2006
Ken Howard/Metropolitan Opera

Ramón Vargas as Rodolfo and Angela Gheorghiu as Mimì, 2008
Marty Sohl/Metropolitan Opera

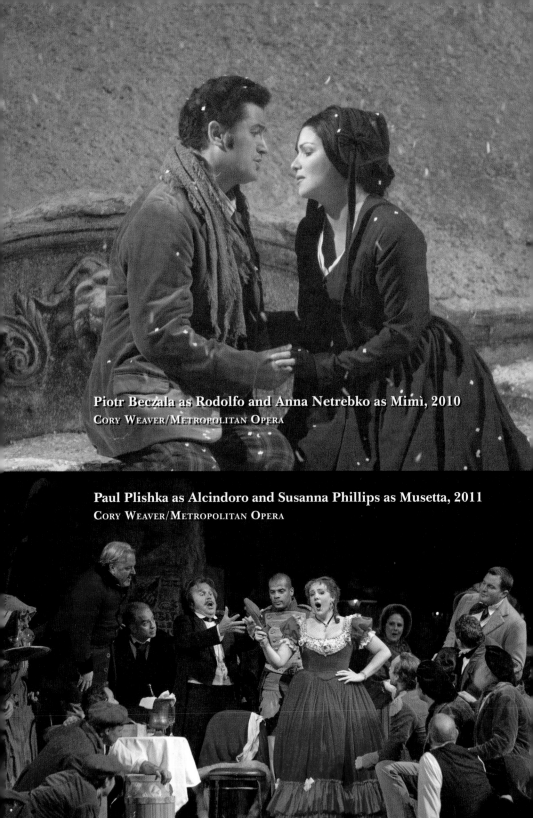

Piotr Beczala as Rodolfo and Anna Netrebko as Mimì, 2010
CORY WEAVER/METROPOLITAN OPERA

Paul Plishka as Alcindoro and Susanna Phillips as Musetta, 2011
CORY WEAVER/METROPOLITAN OPERA

MARCELLO
Bada, sotto il mio cappello non ci stan certi ornamenti...³
Mind you, under my hat not there are certain ornaments...
(Mind you, under my hat certain ornaments don't go!)

MUSETTA
Io detesto quegli amanti che la fanno da mariti.
I detest those lovers who behave like husbands!

MIMÌ, RODOLFO
Chiacchieran le fontane. La brezza della sera
Chatter the fountains. The breeze of the evening

balsami stende sulle doglie umane.
balms spreads over the sufferings human.
(The evening breeze spreads balm over human suffering.)

MARCELLO
Io non faccio da zimbello
I won't play the laughingstock

ai novizi intraprendenti.
to novices enterprising.
(to enterprising novices.)

MUSETTA
Fo all'amor con chi mi piace! Non ti garba?
I make love with whom I please! Not you it suits?

MARCELLO
Vana, frivola civetta!
Vain, frivolous flirt!

Ve ne andate? Vi ringrazio, or son ricco divenuto.

Are you going? I thank you, now I have rich become.

(Are you going? Good! Thanks! I feel richer for it!)

MUSETTA

Musetta se ne va, sì!

Musetta's going away, yes!

MUSETTA, MARCELLO

Vi saluto.

To you I bid good-bye!

MIMÌ, RODOLFO

Vuoi che aspettiam la primavera ancor?

Do you want that we wait for the spring again?

(Do you want us to wait for spring again?)

MUSETTA

Signor, addio vi dico con piacer!

Sir, good-bye to you I say with pleasure!

(Sir, I say good-bye to you with pleasure!)

MARCELLO

Son servo,[4] e me ne vo!

I'm your servant and I'm going away!

(I obey you and am leaving!)

MUSETTA

(Lei si spegne furiosamente ma poi shes improvvisamente si ferma e grida velenosamente a lui:)

(She goes off furiously but then suddenly shes stops and shouts venomously at him:)

Pittore da bottega!
Painter of store!
(You hack house painter!)

MARCELLO
Vipera!
Viper!

MUSETTA
Rospo!
Toad!

MARCELLO
Strega!
Witch!

MIMÌ
Sempre tua per la vita.
Always yours for (the) life.

MIMÌ, RODOLFO
Ci lascieremo alla stagion dei fior!
We'll leave each other at the season of flowers!

(Entrambi, vanno lontano. Marcello restituisce alla taverna.)
(They go off. Marcello returns to the tavern.)

MIMÌ
Vorrei che eterno durasse il verno!
I would like that eternal lasted the winter!
(I would like winter to last eternally!)

MIMÌ, RODOLFO
Ci lascierem alla stagion dei fior!
We'll leave each other at the season of flowers!

FINE DI ATTO III
END OF ACT III

ATTO QUARTO
ACT IV

In soffitta
In the garret

(Marcello di nuovo al cavalletto. Rodolfo al tavolo. Vorrebbero lavorare, ma non fanno che chiacchierare.)
(As in Act I. Marcello is once more before his easel and Rodolfo is seated at his table. They would like to convince each other that they are seriously at work, whereas in reality, they do nothing but chat.)

MARCELLO
(continuando il discorso)
(continuing the conversation)
In un coupé?
In a coupé?[1]

RODOLFO
Con pariglia e livree.
With a pair and livery.
(With a pair of horses and liveried coachmen.)

Mi salutò ridendo.
Me she greeted laughing.
(She greeted me, laughing.)

Tò, Musetta! le dissi:
Why, Musetta! I said to her:

E il cuor? "Non batte o non lo sento
And the heart? "It doesn't beat, or not it I feel
(And your heart? "It doesn't beat, or I do not feel it…)

grazie al velluto che il copre."
thanks to the velvet that it covers."
(thanks to the rich velvet clothes that cover it.")

MARCELLO
Ci ho gusto davver.
I am delighted over it truly!

RODOLFO
(fra se)
(to himself)
(Loiola² va. Ti rodi e ridi.)
(Hypocrite, go on. You're consumed and you laugh.)

MARCELLO
(ruminare)
(ruminating)
Non batte? Bene! Io pur vidi…
Doesn't beat? Good! I also saw…

RODOLFO
Musetta?

MARCELLO
Mimì.

RODOLFO
(Si rabbrividisce.)
(He shudders.)
L'hai vista?
You've seen her?

(fingendo noncuranza)
(then composing himself)

Oh guarda!
Well look at that!…

MARCELLO
Era in carrozza vestita come una regina.
She was in (a) carriage dressed like a queen.

RODOLFO
Evviva! Ne son contento.
Hurrah! About it I am happy.
(Hurrah! I am happy about it.)

MARCELLO
(fra se)
(to himself)
(Bugiardo, si strugge d'amor.)
(Liar, he's consumed with love.)

RODOLFO, MARCELLO
Lavoriam.
Let's work.

(Si mettono al lavoro, ma subito gettano penna e pennello.)
(They start to work.)

RODOLFO
(getta la penna)
(throwing down his pen)
Che penna infame!
What pen terrible!
(What a terrible pen!)

MARCELLO
(getta il pennello)
(throwing down his brush)
Che infame pennello!
What (a) terrible brush!

RODOLFO
O Mimì, tu più non torni, o giorni belli,
Oh Mimì, you more not return, oh days beautiful,
(Oh Mimì, you return no more, oh beautiful days,)

piccole mani, odorosi capelli...
tiny hands, fragrant hair...

collo di neve! Ah! Mimì, mia breve gioventù!
neck of snow! Ah! Mimì, my brief youth!
(white neck just like snow!)

MARCELLO
Io non so come sia che il mio pennello lavori
I don't know how it is that my brush works

e impasti colori contro voglia mia.
and mixes colors against (the) will mine.
(and mixes colors against my will.)

Se pingere mi piace o cieli o terre
If painting I like or skies or lands
(If I like painting skies or landscapes)

o inverni o primavere,
or winters or springs,

egli mi traccia due pupille nere
it for me draws two pupils black
(my brush draws two black eyes for me)

e una bocca procace.
and a mouth provocative.

E n'esce di Musetta il viso ancor…
And out comes of Musetta the face again…
(And out comes the face of Musetta again)

tutto vezzi e tutto frode.
all charm and all deceit.

Musetta intanto gode,
Musetta meanwhile enjoys herself,

e il mio cuor vile la chiama,
and my heart cowardly her calls,
(and my cowardly heart is calling for her,)

la chiama e aspetta il vil mio cuor.
her calls and awaits the cowardly my heart.
(my cowardly heart calls her and waits for her.)

RODOLFO
E tu, cuffietta lieve, che sotto il guancial
And you, bonnet light, which under the pillow

partendo ascose, tutta sai la nostra felicità,
as she left she hid, all you know our happiness,
(And you, little light bonnet which she hid under the pillow before
she left, you know our entire happiness,)

vien sul mio cor morto; ah vien poiché è morto amor.
come upon my heart dead; ah come since is dead love.
(come, little bonnet I place you upon my dead heart, since love is
dead.)

Che ora sia?
What time can it be?

MARCELLO
L'ora del pranzo...di ieri!
Time for dinner...yesterday's!

RODOLFO
E Schaunard non torna?
And Schaunard isn't back?

(Schaunard entra. Colline è con lui.)
(Schaunard and Colline enter.)

SCHAUNARD
(posa quattro pagnotte sulla tavola)
(setting four loaves on the table)
Eccoci!
Here we are!

RODOLFO
Ebben?
Well?

MARCELLO
(con sprezzo)
(with disdain)
Ebben? Del pan?
Well? Some bread?

COLLINE
(mostrando un aringa.)
(showing a herring)
È un piatto degno di Demostene: Un'aringa…
It is a dish worthy of Demosthenes:[3] A herring!

SCHAUNARD
…salata!
…salty!

COLLINE
Il pranzo è in tavola.
The dinner is on the table.

(Si seggono. Siedono a tavola, fingendo d'essere ad un lauto pranzo.)
(They all sit around the table, making believe they are at a sumptuous dinner.)

MARCELLO
Questa è cuccagna da Berlingaccio.[4]
This is abundance of Shrove Thursday.
(This is an abundance worthy of Shrove Thursday.)

SCHAUNARD
(Mette la bottiglia d'acqua nel cappello di Colline.)
(He puts Colline's hat on the table and sets a bottle of water in it.)
Ora lo sciampagna mettiamo in ghiaccio.
Now the champagne we'll put on ice.

RODOLFO
(a Marcello)
(to Marcello)
Scelga, o Barone, trota o salmone?
Choose, oh Baron, trout or salmon?

MARCELLO
(a Schaunard)
(to Schaunard)
Duca, una lingua di pappagallo?
Duke, a tongue of parrot?

SCHAUNARD
Grazie, m'impingua, stasera ho un ballo.
Thanks, it's fattening. Tonight I have a ball.
(No thanks, it's fattening. This evening I'm going to a ball.)

(Colline si alza.)
(Colline has eaten and rises.)

RODOLFO
(a Colline)
(to Colline)
Già sazio?
Already sated?

COLLINE
(con importanza e gravità)
(solemnly)
Ho fretta. Il Re m'aspetta.
I'm in a hurry. The King awaits me.

MARCELLO
C'è qualche trama?
Is there some plot?

RODOLFO, SCHAUNARD, MARCELLO
Qualche mister?
Some mystery?

COLLINE
Il Re mi chiama al minister.
The King me calls to the ministry.
(The King is calling me to the ministry.[5])

SCHAUNARD, MARCELLO, RODOLFO
Bene!
Good!

COLLINE
(con aria di protezione)
(with importance)
Però vedrò…Guizot![6]
However I'll see…Guizot!

SCHAUNARD
(a Marcello)
(to Marcello)
Porgimi il nappo!
Hand me the goblet!

MARCELLO
(dandogli il solo vetro)
(giving him the only glass)
Sì! Bevi, io pappo.
Yes! Drink; I'm feeding!

SCHAUNARD
(solennemente)
(solemnly)
Mi sia permesso al nobile consess...
May I be permitted by the noble company...

RODOLFO, COLLINE
(interrompendolo)
(interrupting him)
Basta!
Enough!

MARCELLO
(dopo aver assaggiato la bevanda)
(after having tasted the drink)
Fiacco!
Weak!

COLLINE
Che decotto!
What (a) concoction!

MARCELLO
Leva il taco!
Lift the heel!
(Lift your heels! Get out!)

COLLINE
Dammi il gotto!
Give me the goblet!

SCHAUNARD
(ispirato)
(inspired)
M'ispira irresistibile l'estro della romanza!
I'm inspired irresistibly (by) the genius of song!

GLI ALTRI
THE OTHERS
(urlando)
(shouting)
No!

SCHAUNARD
(umilmente)
(meekly)
Azione coreografica allora?
Action choreographic then?
(Some choreographic action then?)

GLI ALTRI
THE OTHERS
(applaudendo)
(applauding)
Sì!
Yes!

SCHAUNARD
La danza con musica vocale!
The dance with music vocal!
(The dance, accompanied by vocal music!)

COLLINE
Si sgombrino le sale.
May they be cleared the halls!
(Let the halls be cleared!)

(Portano da un lato la tavola e le sedie e si dispongono a ballare.)
(They carry the table and chairs to one side and prepare themselves to dance.)

Gavotta.
Gavotte.

MARCELLO
Minuetto.
Minuet.

RODOLFO
Pavanella.
Pavane.

SCHAUNARD
Fandango.
Fandango.

COLLINE
Propongo la quadriglia.
I propose the quadrille.

RODOLFO
Mano alle dame!
Hand to the ladies!
(Give your hand to the ladies!)

COLLINE
Io detto.
I'll call.

SCHAUNARD
Lallera, lallera, là...là
Tra-la-lara-la...

RODOLFO
(galante a Marcello)
(gallantly to Marcello)
Vezzosa damigella...
Charming damsel...

MARCELLO
Rispetti la modestia. La prego.
Respect the modesty. I beg you.

SCHAUNARD
Lallera, lallera etc.

COLLINE
Balancez!
Balancez![7]

MARCELLO
Lallera, etc.

SCHAUNARD
Prima c'è il *Rond*.
First there is the *Rond*.
(First we'll have a *Rond* dance.)

COLLINE
No! Bestia.
No! Animal!

SCHAUNARD
Che modi da lacchè!
What manners of a lackey!

COLLINE
Se non erro lei m'oltraggia.
If I'm not mistaken you're insulting me!

(Egli prende la pinza del fuoco.)
(He takes the fire tongs.)

Snudi il ferro!
Unsheathe the steel!
(Unsheathe your sword!)

SCHAUNARD
(Prende la paletta del camino e mettendosi in posizione per battersi.)
(He takes the shovel and starts wielding blows with it.)
Pronti. Assaggia. Il tuo sangue voglio ber.
Ready. Taste that! Your blood I want to drink!

COLLINE
(combattimento)
(fighting)
Un di noi qui si sbudella.
One of us here gets disemboweled.

SCHAUNARD
Apprestate una barella.
Make ready a stretcher.

COLLINE
Apprestate un cimiter.
Make ready a cemetery.

(Mentre combattono, Marcello e Rodolfo danza intorno a loro canto.)
(While they fight, Marcello and Rodolfo dance around them singing.)

RODOLFO, MARCELLO
Mentre incalza la tenzone gira e balza Rigodone...[8]
While rages the combat, turns and leap rigadoon...
(While the combat rages, we turn and leap in a rigadoon.)

(La porta si spalanca ed entra Musetta molto agitato.)
(The door flies open and Musetta enters greatly agitated.)

MARCELLO
(ha colpito)
(struck)
Musetta!

(Tutti rimangono storditi.)
(All remain stunned.)

MUSETTA
(ansimante)
(gasping)
C'è Mimì...che mi segue e che sta male.
There's Mimì...who me follows and who is ill.
(There's Mimì who is following me and she is very sick.)

RODOLFO
(atterrito)
(terrified)

Ov'è?
Where is she?

MUSETTA
Nel far le scale più non si resse.
In climbing the stairs, more not could she bear it.
(As she climbed the stairs, she could no longer bear it and her strength failed her.)

(Si vede, per l'uscio aperto, Mimì seduta sul più alto gradino della scala.)
(One can see through the open door Mimì sitting on the last step of the stairs.)

RODOLFO
Ah!

(Si precipita verso Mimì.)
(He runs to Mimì.)

SCHAUNARD
(a Colline)
(to Colline)
Noi accostiamo quel lettuccio.
We'll move closer that cot.

(Ambedue portano innanzi il letto.)
(With Marcello's help, Rodolfo leads Mimì towards the cot where he helps her lie down.)

RODOLFO
(dopo aver impostato Mimì giù, sottovoce per gli amici)
(after setting Mimì down, softly to his friends)
Là...Da bere.
There...Something to drink.

(Musetta accorre col bicchiere dell'acqua e ne dà un sorso a Mimì.)
(Musetta comes with a glass of water and gives it to Mimì.)

MIMÌ
(recuperando, e vedendo Rodolfo accanto a lei)
(recovering, and seeing Rodolfo near her)
Rodolfo!

RODOLFO
Zitta riposa.
Hush, rest.

MIMÌ
O mio Rodolfo! Mi vuoi qui con te?
Oh my Rodolfo! Do you want me here with you?

RODOLFO
(Le fa segno con amore a lei di tacere, rimanere accanto a lei.)
(He lovingly motions to her to be silent, remaining near her.)
Ah! Mia Mimì, sempre, sempre!
Ah! My Mimì, always, always!

MUSETTA
(agli altri, piano)
(to Marcello, Schaunard and Colline, softly)
Intesi dire che Mimì, fuggita dal Viscontino,
I heard it said that Mimì, having fled from the Viscount,

era in fin di vita.
was at the end of life.
(was near death.)

Dove stia? Cerca…La veggo passar per via…
Where could she be? I searched…Her I see passing in the street…
(Where could she be? I searched…and then I see her passing in
the street…)

trascinandosi a stento. Mi dice: "Più non reggo…
dragging herself barely. To me she says: "No more can I bear it…

muoio, lo sento. Voglio morir con lui! Forse m'aspetta…!"
I'm dying, I feel it. I want to die with him! Maybe he's waiting for
me…!"

MIMÌ
Mi sento assai meglio…
I feel much better…

MUSETTA
"M'accompagni, Musetta?"
"Will you accompany me, Musetta?…"

MIMÌ
Lascia ch'io guardi intorno.
Let that I look around.
(Let me look around.)

Ah, come si sta bene qui!
Ah, how one is comfortable here!

Si rinasce. Ancor sento la vita qui…
One is reborn. Again I feel (the) life here…

No, tu non mi lasci più!
No, you won't me leave anymore!
(No, you won't leave me anymore!)

RODOLFO
Benedetta bocca, tu ancor mi parli!
Blessed mouth, you're again to me speaking!
(Blessed mouth, you are speaking to me again!)

MUSETTA
(da parte agli altri tre)
(to the three)
Che ci avete in casa?
What do you have at home?

MARCELLO
Nulla!
Nothing!

MUSETTA
Non caffè? Non vino?
No coffee? No wine?

MARCELLO
Nulla! Ah! Miseria!
Nothing! Ah! Poverty!

SCHAUNARD
(osservata cautamente Mimì, tristemente a Colline, traendolo in disparate)
(sadly to Colline, taking him aside)
Fra mezz'ora è morta!
In a half hour she's dead!

MIMÌ
Ho tanto freddo…Se avessi un manicotto!
I have so much cold…If I had a muff!
(I'm so cold…If only I had a muff!)

Queste mie mani riscaldare non si potranno mai?
These my hands warm not themselves can they ever?
(These hands of mine, can they ever get warm?)

(Tossisce.)
(She coughs.)

RODOLFO
(prendendole le mani nelle sue, scaldarle)
(taking her hands in his, warming them)
Qui nelle mie! Taci, il parlar ti stanca.
Here in mine! Hush, talking you tires.
(Here, warm them in my hands! Hush, talking makes you tired.)

MIMÌ
Ho un po' di tosse! Ci sono avvezza.
I have a little (of) cough! To it I am accustomed.
(I have a little cough! I am used to it.)

(Vedendo gli amici di Rodolfo, li chiama per nome: essi accorrono premurosi presso di lei.)
(Seeing Rodolfo's friends, she calls them by name; they all concernedly rush to Mimì's side.)

Buon giorno, Marcello, Schaunard, Colline, buon giorno.
Good day, Marcello, Schaunard, Colline, good day.

Tutti qui, tutti qui sorridenti a Mimì.
All here smiling at Mimì.

RODOLFO
Non parlar.
Don't talk.

MIMÌ
Parlo pian, non temere.
I'm speaking softly, do not fear.

Marcello, date retta: È assai buona Musetta.
Marcello, pay heed: She's very good (your) Musetta.

MARCELLO
(porge la mano a Musetta)
(holding out his hand to Musetta)
Lo so.
I know.

MUSETTA
(dà gli orecchini a Marcello)
(taking off her earrings and handing them to Marcello)
A te...vendi, riporta qualche cordial,
Here...sell them, bring back some cordial,

manda un dottore!
send a doctor!

RODOLFO
Riposa.
Rest.

MIMÌ
Tu non mi lasci?
You aren't me leaving?
(You aren't leaving me?)

RODOLFO
No! No!

MUSETTA
(a Marcello chi si affretta fuori per ottenere la bevanda)
(to Marcello who is hurrying off to get the cordial)
Ascolta! Forse è l'ultima volta
Listen! Perhaps it's the last time

che ha espresso un desiderio, poveretta!
that she's expressed a desire, poor thing!

Pel manicotto io vo. Con te verrò.
For the muff I'm going. With you I'll come.
(I'm going to get the muff. I'll go with you.)

MARCELLO
(commosso)
(moved)
Sei buona, o mia Musetta.
You're good, oh my Musetta.

COLLINE
(levandosi il pastrano)
(who has taken off his coat while Marcello and Musetta were speaking)
Vecchia zimarra, senti,
Old coat, listen,

io resto al pian, tu ascendere
I'm staying on the ground, you climb

il sacro monte or devi.
the holy mountain now you must.
(I am staying below but you must go up to the sacred mountain.[9])

Le mie grazie ricevi.
My thanks receive.
(Receive my thanks.)

Mai non curvasti il logoro dorso
Never not you bowed the worn back

ai ricchi ed ai potenti.
to the rich and to the powerful.

Passar nelle tue tasche
There passed through your pockets

come in antri tranquilli filosofi e poeti.
as in grottoes tranquil philosophers and poets.
(Philosophers and poets passed through your pockets as if through
tranquil grottoes.)

Ora che i giorni lieti fuggir,
Now that the days happy have fled,

ti dico addio, fedele amico mio, addio.
to you I say farewell, faithful friend of mine, farewell.

(Mette l'involto sotto il braccio, poi dice sottovoce a Schaunard:)
(Having made a bundle, he puts it under his arm, but seeing Schaunard,
he tells him softly:)

Schaunard, ognuno per diversa via
Schaunard, each one in a different way

mettiamo insieme due atti di pieta:
let's combine together two acts of mercy:

Io...qusto!
I...this!

(Gli mostra la zimarra che tiene sotto il braccio e punti a Rodolfo e Mimì.)
(He shows him the coat under his arm and points to Rodolfo and Mimì.)

E tu...lasciali soli là!
And you leave them alone there.

SCHAUNARD
(commosso)
(moved)
Filosofo, ragioni! È ver...Vo via!
Philosopher, you're reasoning. It's true...I'm leaving!

(Escono.)
(He looks around and then follows Colline, carefully closing the door.)

MIMÌ
Sono andati? Fingevo di dormire
Are they gone? I pretended to sleep

perché volli con te sola restare.
because I wanted with you alone to remain.

Ho tante cose che ti voglio dire
I've so many things that to you I want to say
(I've so many things that I want to say to you)

o una sola ma grande come il mare.
or one only, but big as the sea.

Come il mare profonda ed infinita
Like the sea deep and infinite

ei il mio amor, e tutta la mia vita.
you are my love, and all my life.

RODOLFO
Ah Mimì, mia bella Mimì!
Ah Mimì, my beautiful Mimì!

MIMÌ
Son bella ancora?
Am I beautiful still?

RODOLFO
Bella come un'aurora…
Beautiful like a dawn…

MIMÌ
Hai sbagliato il raffronto,
You have mistaken the comparison,

volevi dir: bella come un tramonto.
you meant to say: beautiful like a sunset.

"Mi chiamano Mimì, il perché non so."
"Me they call Mimì, the reason I don't know."

RODOLFO
(intenerito e carezzevole)
(tender and caressing)
Tornò al nido la rondine e cinguetta.
Returned to the nest the swallow and is twittering.
(The swallow has returned to its nest and is twittering.)

(Leva la cuffietta di dove l'aveva riposta in sul cuore.)
(He takes Mimì's bonnet, which he had over his heart, and hands it to her.)

MIMÌ
(gaiamente)
(radiant)
La mia cuffietta...
My bonnet...

(Tende a Rodolfo la testa, questi le mette la cuffietta. Mimì fa sedere presso a lei Rodolfo e rimane colla testa appoggiata sul petto di lui.)
(She holds her head towards Rodolfo, who puts the bonnet on it. Mimì stays with her head leaning on his chest.)

Ah! te lo rammenti
Ah! Do you remember

quando sono entrata la prima volta, là?
when I came in the first time, there?

RODOLFO
Se lo rammento...
If it I remember....
(If I remember it...)

MIMÌ
Il lume s'era spento...
The fire had gone out...

RODOLFO
Eri tanto turbata!
You were so upset!

Poi smarristi la chiave…
Then you lost the key…

MIMÌ
E a cercarla tastoni ti sei messo.
And to look for it groping you began.
(And you began groping looking for it.)

RODOLFO
E cerca…cerca…
And I looked…I looked…

MIMÌ
Mio bel signorino, posso ben dirlo adesso,
My fine young gentleman, I can well say it now,

lei la trovò assai presto.
you it found much too quickly.
(you found the key quickly enough.)

RODOLFO
Aiutavo il destino.
I was helping (the) destiny.

MIMÌ
(ricordando l'incontro suo con Rodolfo la sera della vigilia di Natale)
(remembering her meeting with Rodolfo on Christmas Eve)
Era buio e il mio rossor non si vedeva…
It was dark and my blushing not was seen…
(It was dark and you couldn't see me blushing.)

(Sussurra le parole di Rodolfo.)
(She murmurs Rodolfo's words.)

"Che gelida manina, se la lasci riscaldar!"
"What icy little hand, let it be warmed!"

Era buio e la man tu mi prendevi...
It was dark and the hand you me took...
(It was dark and you took my hand...)

(Mimì è presa da uno spasimo di soffocazione.)
(Mimì is overcome by a choking fit and she lets her head fall, exhausted.)

RODOLFO
(spaventati)
(frightened)
Oh Dio! Mimì!
Oh God! Mimì!

(Schaunard rientra in quel momento.)
(At this moment Schaunard returns. At Rodolfo's scream, he runs towards Mimì.)

SCHAUNARD
Che avvien?
What's happening?

MIMÌ
(Apre gli occhi e sorride per rassicurare Rodolfo e Schaunard.)
(She opens her eyes and smiles to reassure Rodolfo and Schaunard.)
Nulla, sto bene.
Nothing, I'm all right.

RODOLFO
Zitta, per carità.
Hush, for pity's sake.

MIMÌ
Si, si, perdona, or sarò buona.
Yes, yes, forgive me, now I'll be good.

(Tornano Marcello e Musetta, poi Colline. Musetta pone un lume sulla tavola.)
(Marcello and Musetta enter, she with a muff and he with a phial.)

MUSETTA
(a Rodolfo)
(to Rodolfo)
Dorme?
Is she asleep?

RODOLFO
Riposa.
She's resting.

MARCELLO
Ho veduto il dottore: Verrà;
I've seen the doctor: He'll come;

gli ho fatto fretta. Ecco il cordial.
I told him to hurry. Here's the cordial.

(Prende una lampada a spirito, la pone sulla tavola e l'accende.)
(He takes a spirit lamp, lights it and places it on the table.)

MIMÌ
Chi parla?
Who's talking?

MUSETTA
(Lei si avvicina a Mimì e porge il manicotto)
(She comes close to Mimì and hands her the muff)
Io, Musetta.
I, Musetta.

MIMÌ
Oh, come è bello e morbido.
Oh, how it's lovely and soft.

Non più le mani allividite.
No more the hands pale.
(No more pale hands.)

Il tepore le abbellirà.
The warmth them will beautify.
(The warmth will make them beautiful.)

(a Rodolfo)
(to Rodolfo)

Sei tu che me lo doni?
Is it you who me it gives?
(Is it you who gives it to me?)

MUSETTA
(pronta)
(promptly)
Sì.
Yes.

MIMÌ
Tu! Spensierato! Grazie. Ma costerà.
You, carefree one! Thank you. But it must cost.
(You spendthrift, thank you, but it must have cost a lot.)

(Rodolfo scoppia in pianto.)
(Rodolfo begins to weep.)

Piangi? Sto bene... pianger così perché?
You're crying? I'm well...to cry thus why?
(You're crying? I'm well...why do you cry like this?)

(Ella appisola a poco a poco.)
(She dozes off little by little.)

Qui, amor...sempre con te...!
Here, love...always with you...!

Le mani...al caldo...e...dormire...*(silenzio)*
The hands...in the warmth...and...to sleep...*(silence)*

RODOLFO
(a Marcello)
(to Marcello)
Che ha detto il medico?
What has said the doctor?
(What did the doctor say?)

MARCELLO
Verrà.
He'll come.

MUSETTA
*(Fa scaldare la medicina portata da Marcello sul fornello a spirito,
e quasi inconsciamente mormora una preghiera.)*
*(She warms the phial at the spirit lamp and almost unconsciously murmurs
a prayer.)*
Madonna benedetta,
Madonna blessed,
(Blessed Mother,)

fate la grazia a questa poveretta
be merciful to this poor girl

che non debba morire.
that not she must die.
(so that she won't have to die.)

(interrompendosi, a Marcello)
(interrupting herself, to Marcello)

Qui ci vuole un riparo, perché la fiamma sventola.
Here we need a screen, because the flame is flickering.

(Marcello mette un libro sulla tavola da paravento al lume.)
(Marcello sets a book upright on the table, forming a screen for the lamp.)

Così.
Like that.

(Ripiglia la preghiera.)
(She resumes the prayer.)

E che possa guarire.
And that she may get well.

Madonna santa, io sono indegna di perdono,
Mother holy, I am not worthy of forgiveness,

mentre invece Mimì è un angelo del cielo.
while instead Mimì is an angel from Heaven.

(Mentre Musetta prega, Rodolfo le si è avvicinato.)
(While Musetta is praying Rodolfo comes over to her.)

RODOLFO
Io spero ancora. Vi pare che sia grave?
I hope still. Do you think that it's serious?
(I still have hope.)

MUSETTA
Non credo.
I don't believe so.

(Schaunard s'avvicina al letto.)
(Schaunard has come close to the couch, then without attracting attention goes over to Marcello.)

SCHAUNARD
(piano a Marcello)
(softly to Marcello)
Marcello, è spirata…
Marcello, she has expired…

(Intanto Rodolfo si è avveduto che il sole della finestra della soffitta sta per battere sul volto di Mimì e cerca intorno come porvi riparo; Musetta se ne avvede e gli indica la sua mantiglia, sale su di una sedia e studia il modo di distenderla sulla finestra. Marcello si avvicina a sua volta al letto e se ne scosta atterrito; intanto entra Colline che depone del danaro sulla tavola presso a Musetta.)
(Meanwhile Rodolfo realizes that the sun coming in from the window is about to fall on Mimì's face and searches around for a way to prevent this. Musetta notices and points to her shawl. Rodolfo thanks her with a glance and takes the shawl and getting up on a chair tries to somehow hang it over the window. Marcello nears the cot and moves away, frightened. Meanwhile Colline enters and puts the money on the table near Musetta.)

COLLINE
(entra e dà del danaro a Musetta)
(giving some money to Musetta)
Musetta…a voi!
Musetta…for you!

(Poi visto Rodolfo che solo non riesce a collocare la mantiglia corre ad aiutarlo chiedendogli di Mimì)
(Then seeing that Rodolfo by himself isn't able to manage the shawl over the window, he runs to help him, asking him about Mimì.)

Come va?
How is she?

RODOLFO
Vedi? È tranquilla.
You see? She's calm.

(Rodolfo si accorge dello strano contegno degli altri.)
(He turns towards Mimì. At that moment Musetta gives him a signal that the medicine is ready. Rodolfo, as he rushes to Musetta, notices the strange attitude of Marcello and Schaunard, who, filled with dismay, look at him with profound pity.)

Che vuol dire? Quell'andare e venire…
What does it mean that going and coming…

quel guardarmi così…?
that looking at me like that…?

(Non regge più, corre a Rodolfo e abbracciandolo con voce angosciata grida:)
(Marcello can't restrain himself anymore and runs to Rodolfo, embracing him and murmuring in a suffocated voice:)

MARCELLO
Coraggio!
Courage!

RODOLFO
(accorre al lettuccio)
(Finally understanding, he runs to the cot.)
Mimì!

FINE DEL OPERA
END OF THE OPERA

NOTES

ACT I

1 The implication here is that all the wood (forests) is lying under the snows of winter and unavailable to the Bohemians for firewood.

2 *Freddo cane*, lit. "cold dog" (I am dog cold). Very, very cold.

3 The reference is to Louis Philippe, the reigning monarch of France at the time, whose likeness appears on the coins.

4 *Mabille* was a well-known French cabaret in Paris at the time of the action.

5 It is difficult to adequately translate this Italian play on words. The librettists indulged themselves in a bit of punning by changing the *arzillo* and *pettoruto* words in the line above to *arzuto e pettorillo*, transposing the "*illo*" and "*uto*" endings.

6 The "troubling" quality implied is cuckoldry. The **horns** allusion here refers to the horns of the cuckold, which grow *sopra capi* "above the head."

7 Burning sugar conceivably cleansed the air of rank odors and impurities created by the presence of the womanizing and profligate Benoit!

8 A well-known café in Paris's Latin Quarter (*Quartiere Latino*), on the left bank of the river Seine, gathering spot for all Bohemians and artists.

ACT II

1 Runic grammars deal with the languages of ancient northern European peoples.
2 Ratafià is a liqueur made from the juice of wild cherries, sugar and alcohol.
3 Horace was a Roman poet and satirist who lived 65–9 BC. He was educated in Rome and Athens. He received patronage of Maecenas and was given a villa in Rome in the Sabine Hills. He also enjoyed the favor of Emperor Augustus. Due to his exalted station in society, he looked down on the common people.
4 From hanging around Colline, the philosopher, the boys have picked up a bit of Latin, and Schaunard is just trying to sound erudite in front of the new guest (Mimì).
5 The children here are talking of toy soldiers, of course.
6 *al tu per tu* means in an intimate setting where Italians speak to each other in the familiar *tu* form rather than the more formal *voi* or *lei*.
7 The allusion by Rodolfo is that angels go naked, so that Musetta (being no angel) is fully dressed to the hilt.
8 *civetta* in Italian means both "screech owl" and "coquette."
9 Sucking honey in this case implies that Marcello, although on one level reacting in misery to Musetta's antics, is also **finding it sweet**, the fact that she has searched him out.

ACT III

1 *aver l'ossa rotte*, to "have broken bones," meaning "to be dead tired."
2 *acconciare uno pel di delle feste*, literally "to thrash someone for a feast day" meaning nothing to an English speaker, but to an

Italian an idiomatic expression meaning "to give someone a severe thrashing."

3   *ornamenti* (ornaments) refers to the horns of the cuckold.

4   *son servo* is an old expression which meant "at your service" or I'm your servant," all expressions implying obedience. It comes from the Latin *Servus*. In Austrian German it has survived as *servus* to mean "hello," "goodbye," or even "fancy seeing you here!"

ACT IV

1   *coupé*, in French means "cut." It was applied in olden times to carriages which were "cut" or having a smaller enclosure for the passenger. We use the same name in America and refer to a *coupe*, usually a two-door car, in contrast to a sedan (named after the sedan chairs or litters), which is a larger, usually four-door car.

2   The reason *Loiola* means hypocrite stems from the fact that Saint Ignatius of Loyola, the founder of the Jesuits, was considered by the rank and file of Catholic clergy as a renegade who spoke of one thing (Catholicism) but meant something else (Jesuit reforms). The term *Loiola* or *loiolesco* had acquired this connotation in the Italian of Puccini's era.

3   Demosthenes: the most famous Greek orator (385–322 B.C.).

4   *Berlingaccio*: Last Thursday of Carnival, when people feast just before the beginning of Lent.

5   "ministry" in the sense of a Government department, not a clerical appointment by the King.

6   Guizot: Louis Philippe's prime minister at the time.

7   *balancez*: Ballet term meaning "balance yourself."

8   *rigodone* (In French *Rigaudon*): a spirited dance believed to have originated in French Provence and named after its inventor, a certain Rigaud.

9 *sacro monte* (sacred mountain) refers to the *monte pietà* or pawn-shop district, where Colline wants to pawn his coat in order to get some money to help Mimì.